DREAMING BEYOND DEATH

A Guide to Pre-Death Dreams and Visions

~

KELLY BULKELEY, PH.D., AND THE
REVEREND PATRICIA BULKLEY

Beacon Press, Boston

BEACON PRESS
Boston, Massachusetts
www.beacon.org

Beacon Press books
are published under the auspices of
the Unitarian Universalist Association of Congregations.

19 18 17 16   8 7 6 5 4 3 2

This book is printed on acid-free paper that meets the uncoated paper
ANSI/NISO specifications for permanence as revised in 1992.

Text design by Patricia Duque Campos
Composition by Wilsted & Taylor Publishing Services

Library of Congress Cataloging-in-Publication Data

Bulkeley, Kelly
Dreaming beyond death : a guide to pre-death dreams and visions / Kelly
Bulkeley and Patricia Bulkley.
p. cm.
Includes bibliographical references and index.
ISBN 978-0-8070-7715-3 (pbk. : acid-free paper)
1. Death in dreams. 2. Dream interpretation.
I. Bulkley, Patricia. II. Title.

BF1099.D4B85 2005
154.6'32—dc22
2004024186

To TRACY MOLONY
And all the generous people who shared their final dreams with us

CONTENTS

INTRODUCTION

Bill, a retired merchant marine ship's captain in his mid-eighties, was diagnosed with bone cancer. A year later the cancer metastasized, and his doctors told him there was nothing more they could do. Knowing that he had just weeks to live, Bill fell into a profound depression. This was it, the end of his life. In just a matter of days he would be dead. Bill felt strangely empty about that prospect. For some reason he didn't really care about anything anymore. Nothing mattered —nothing that had happened in his past, nothing that was happening right now in the few meager hours left to him, and nothing that would happen after he was gone.

And here, in this dark pit of nothingness, Bill realized he did feel something after all. Fear.

Concerned about his worsening condition and emotional distress, Bill's wife asked the hospice organization in charge of his home care if anyone could talk to him and help him with his failing spirits. The hospice staff provided a list of different types of counseling services available, and Bill and his wife discussed the various options. Bill finally decided he wanted to speak with someone who was a minister rather than a secular psychotherapist, since he had found himself thinking in recent days about bits and pieces of his Baptist religious upbringing. Even though he didn't believe much in religion anymore, he thought that perhaps a minister could help him sort things out.

This is how Patricia (henceforth Tish) came to meet Bill. As a Presbyterian minister and spiritual services provider at the hospice taking care of Bill, Tish's job was to visit any patient who had requested to talk with someone about religious or spiritual issues.[1] Tish went to Bill's home, where his wife greeted her and led her to Bill's study. She found Bill sitting alone in a room filled with a lifetime of memories: pictures of ships he had captained, art from the Orient, books, papers, and family photos. The room had a calm, comfortable, lived-in feel to it, but the look on Bill's face was anything but peaceful. He was pale, drawn, and nervous. Tish started the conversation by asking Bill questions about his illness, the level of his physical discomfort, and the likely course of the cancer over the next few days. Then they talked about Bill's wife and what she would do after he was gone. They went on to reflect on dying, and death, and what people believe happens after death, and they discussed the influence of Baptist religious teachings on his life and what he felt about those teachings now. Finally, they considered Paul's words in his second letter to the Corinthians:

> So we do not lose heart. Though our outer nature is wasting away, our inner nature is being renewed every day. For this slight momentary affliction is preparing us for an eternal weight of glory beyond all comparison, because we look not to the things that are seen but to the things that are unseen; for the things that are seen are transient, but the things that are unseen are eternal.[2]

As Tish left she said to Bill, "Perhaps God has that in store for you."

When she returned for another visit a few days later, Tish noticed a remarkable change in Bill's mood and vitality. In striking contrast to his depressed resignation during the previous week's visit, today his eyes were alive with interest, his expression was relaxed, and he was clearly anticipating his conversation with Tish. As soon as she sat down with him in his study, he launched into the following report: "After you left last time I picked up the old family Bible. I remembered for the first time in a long time, spending hours at the helm of my ship feeling all alone in a vast expanse of sea. I used to stand there at the wheel and read aloud out of this old Bible and it helped me feel connected. I knew that God was right there with me, even though we weren't always sure exactly where 'there' was in those days. Last week I had a dream that reminded me of that."

I am sailing again at night in uncharted waters and the old sense of adventure comes back. I feel the tingle of excitement again, of pushing through the waves in the vast, dark, empty sea but knowing somehow I am right on course.

"And strangely enough, I'm not afraid to die anymore. In fact, I feel ready to go, more so every day."

Bill died the next week. At his funeral Tish spoke with Bill's wife, who told Tish that his dream and his change of heart about dying had helped her, too, in giving her the strength to let go even though she missed him terribly and could not imagine what her life would be like without him.

Dreams like this—powerful revelations coming in the last days and hours of a person's life—have been experienced by people throughout history, in cultures all over the world.[3] In most cultures such dreams have been understood as genuine religious experiences in which the dying person begins the transition from this mortal life to whatever state of existence may lie beyond. People in present-day society also experience pre-death dreams with remarkable frequency, although in many cases people today do not know what to make of such strange, visionary occurrences. Living as we do in a culture where scientific authorities assure us that dreaming is nothing more than the random firing of neurons in the brain,[4] people who happen to experience an incredibly powerful pre-death dream often question their own sanity and mental health. They may wonder if their physical illness is damaging their minds and causing the eruption of such bizarre fantasies. Perhaps the medical treatments are to blame, all the high-powered drugs they are being given, or perhaps the dreams are simply the natural by-products of a body shutting down, with no special religious meaning or revelatory significance beyond that. What good, then, could come from paying attention to these dreams? Aren't you going to die anyway?

Yes, death lies inevitably ahead, and having a powerful dream is not going to change that. But the idea that nothing good or valuable can come from people's experiences during those final weeks and days of life reflects a tragically impoverished and shortsighted understanding of what happens when humans die. Our experiences—Tish as a hospice chaplain, Kelly as a dream researcher—have convinced us that pre-death dreams and visions offer gifts of insight and wisdom that can, as in Bill's case, profoundly change a person's view of death and even help his or her friends and family in their time of mourning. We do not pretend to know where these experiences originate, whether in the neural workings of the brain or the fathomless currents of spiritual realities. We do, however, believe an exclusively scientific *or* exclusively religious explanation of pre-death dreams is inadequate. Later in this book we will show why we believe the best understanding of these remarkably widespread experiences comes from an integration of scientific psychology and cross-cultural religious history.

Having said that, our main concern is not with dream theory. Our goal in writing this book has much more to do with

4

the practical consequences of taking pre-death dreams and visions seriously in the care of the dying. Whatever the origin of these experiences may be, what matters is their emotional impact. As a direct result of the dream or vision, the person's fear of death diminishes, and in its place there arises a new understanding of living, dying, and that which lies beyond death. The problem is that too few people in contemporary society have any practical guidance or support in trying to make sense of these potent experiences. We have written *Dreaming Beyond Death* with the intention of providing a clear and accessible resource to help both the dying person and his or her caregivers (including family, friends, clergy, counselors, and medical staff) better understand the mysterious life-changing dreams and visions that come just before the end of mortal life.

We will not claim this is easy to do—sometimes the dream is relatively straightforward, as in Bill's case, but more often than not the experiences involve strange symbolism and puzzling imagery, and quite a few pre-death dreams are so totally bizarre that they seem impossible to interpret or understand. Indeed, people often find it extremely difficult to describe in ordinary language what has happened to them. They struggle to put into words the vividness of the imagery, the intensity of the feelings, and the vibrant *realness* of their sensations. In many cases they cannot say for sure whether it was a dream they experienced, or a vision, or a hallucination, or something else entirely.

The amazing diversity and multiplicity of these experiences does make it challenging to understand them—challenging, but not impossible. In our research we have found a handful of prominent symbolic themes that reappear in pre-death dreams with great frequency, and we hope that describing these themes and highlighting their multiple dimensions of meaning will provide readers with a good foundation for their own practical efforts at understanding pre-death dreams, either their own or those of the people for whom they are caring. We do not promise a simple, one-size-fits-all model for dream interpretation, but rather a flexible set of methods that will help open the dreams to greater conscious awareness. We have developed these methods in both religious contexts (such as pastoral counseling and spiritual direction) and secular contexts (such as psychotherapy and hospital care), and in the pages that follow we will offer a caregiving approach that can be applied in any situation where a person is facing the imminent ending of bodily life.

We start in Chapter 1 with a discussion of different beliefs and practices surrounding dreaming and death in cultures around the world. Learning about the different ways people have understood the intimate connection between dreaming and dying will provide a helpful historical and cross-cultural context in which to explore the dreams of people in present-day society. Our approach, it should be said at the outset, is neither strictly Freudian, in the sense of using free association to decode symbolically disguised wishes, nor strictly Jungian, in the sense of seeking universal archetypes and symbols of the collective unconscious.[5] Rather, we are interested in finding recurrent patterns in people's dreams that reflect widely shared features of human life. In this we are guided by historian of religion Wendy Doniger, who takes a "bottom up" approach to cross-cultural comparisons. In her book *The Implied Spider* she writes, "The method I am advocating . . . assumes certain continuities not about overarching human universals but about particular narrative details concerning the body, sexual desire, procreation, parenting, pain, and death, details which, though unable to avoid mediation by culture entirely, are at least *less* culturally mediated than the broader conceptual categories of the universalists."[6] Following Doniger, the more we can learn about the cross-cultural history of recurrent patterns of dreaming and dying, the better prepared we will be to discern the full range of possibility in people's experiences today.

Chapter 2 provides a summary of the basic principles and

ideas that will guide our discussion of pre-death dreams and visions. These principles are drawn from several sources in contemporary dream research, including psychology, anthropology, neuroscience, and evolutionary biology. To be sure, not all areas of dream research are directly relevant to our interests. Modern Western science has devoted considerable energy over the past 150 years to the examination of dreaming, and much of that work has been aimed at repudiating the value and meaningfulness of dreams (and indeed all nonrational phenomena). Still, despite its materialist and antireligion biases, the scientific study of dreaming can teach us many important things. In Chapter 2 we will focus particular attention on two issues. One regards the anticipatory or rehearsal function of dreaming. Several researchers have provided evidence to support the idea that one of the functions of dreaming is to envision future possibilities in order to prepare the individual for efficient, adaptive action.[7] Seen in this light, pre-death dreams represent the final expression of that anticipatory function, preparing a person for the end of his or her life.

The second issue regards the interpretation of symbols and metaphors in dreams. We will discuss the ideas of cognitive linguist George Lakoff, who has shown how the basic metaphorical operations of the mind are at work in both waking and dreaming life.[8] The essence of metaphorical thinking is to imaginatively portray an *unknown* thing in terms of a *known* thing. In the case of Bill's dream, the metaphor is as simple as it is powerfully evocative: the frightening *unknown* of death is symbolically compared to the alluring *known* of a sea adventure. As strange and bizarre as some dreams may be, careful reflection usually reveals a metaphorical structure of meaning rooted in the current life circumstances of the dreamer. All of the dreams we discuss in this book involve metaphors and symbols by which people envision their impending death in terms of something familiar and known. This is where we can begin to appreciate the endless diversity of pre-death dreams and visions, because each person's dreaming reflects his or her own life history, language, and cultural mythology.

A few common patterns, an infinite variety of metaphorical expressions—both of these characteristics need to be acknowledged, and we show how taking them together provides the basis for a reliable method of interpreting these dreams and deriving practical benefit from them.

In the next three chapters we go into greater detail about the three most prevalent metaphorical themes in pre-death dreams and visions. Chapter 3 discusses dreams in which death is portrayed as a journey. Bill's dream illustrates this theme perfectly, and this is something we have found in numerous other cases. Looking at the many variants of this metaphorical theme of "death as a journey" will show the powerful impact these dreams have in terms of expanding and deepening the dying person's understanding of his or her life story. In Chapter 4 we focus on dreams in which the dreamer meets a guide for the journey, sometimes a religious or spiritual figure and sometimes a trusted person (family member, revered teacher, etc.) who has already died and who has come back to provide help, counsel, and guidance to the dying person. Chapter 5 looks especially closely at the obstacles and challenges people encounter in their pre-death dream journeys, as the different impediments they face are often meaningful expressions of deep anxieties and unresolved conflicts.

In Chapter 6 we bring together all the practical methods we have discussed so far and offer an overall program for caregiving for the dying. Exploring pre-death dreams and visions is best conducted as part of an integrated approach to supporting the dying person's physical, emotional, and spiritual condition. As we have already mentioned, the approach we are offering can be applied in many different caregiving environments, whether religious or secular, and whether by professionals trained in this work or by nonprofessional people such as friends and family members.

The final days of life can be a powerful opportunity to reflect on the story of one's life, particularly on issues and concerns that remain unresolved such as troubled family relationships, unfulfilled desires, long-suppressed frustrations, and fearful uncertainties about religion. Pre-death dreams and visions have a role to play in the integrative process of consciously and deliberately bringing life to a meaningful conclusion. In many cases this process involves an exploration of the person's image of God or, in a less formally religious sense, the person's sense of spiritual powers greater than the self. We have found that many dying people are surprised to find themselves struggling with an image of a harshly judgmental God, and in such situations a dream or vision often comes that can help to transform the person's sense of the divine, easing the guilt-ridden anxiety and bringing a new appreciation of God's presence in the world.

In the conclusion we summarize the practical methods being presented in this book and offer some closing reflections on the historical and cross-cultural prevalence of pre-death dreams and visions. Not everyone has such experiences, but it is clear that all humans have at least the *potential* for them. Every one of us has the seeds of a visionary within.

The inherent human capacity for pre-death dreams and visions is a fact of the utmost importance for the contemporary healthcare system. At the very least, hospital staff and all other professionals trained in care for the dying should be aware that these experiences happen with regularity and are a potentially beneficial resource in practical caregiving work. More than that, new questions need to be raised about the increasing use of psychoactive medications and pain-killing drugs on terminally ill patients. Some of these medications have an inhibiting effect on dreaming, and while no one should suffer needlessly, patients should nevertheless be informed about the adverse impact of such drugs on their capacity for dreaming in the final days of their lives.

Along the same lines, we believe a greater appreciation of pre-death dreams and visions should be included in debates about doctor-assisted suicide. Public discussion about euthanasia is only going to become more urgent in coming years as the baby-boom generation enters old age and new life-support technologies lengthen the duration (but not necessarily the quality) of people's lives. People who suddenly learn they have a fatal illness naturally enough feel an initial sense of panic and terror. In this moment of overwhelming emotion, it often appears the simplest course to end one's life right now, without causing loved ones or oneself any further suffering. What people need to know (and what caregivers need to tell them) is that there are still genuine opportunities for change, growth, and fulfillment in the time (however brief it may be) *after* that initial startling moment of existential fear. An amazing new stage of life opens up as we begin to die, and our hope in this book is to provide a window into the dreaming and visionary experiences that can make this final phase of our bodily existence so richly meaningful.

CHAPTER I

DREAMS OF MORTALITY

Dreaming and Dying

We are all going to die someday. Some of us will die very soon, others not for many years, but we all share the common fate of moving toward an eventual, inescapable ending. The awareness of our mortality makes us human—no other species has the paradoxical curse and blessing of knowing of its own ultimate demise. Even though our conscious attention is usually focused on the busy activities of daily life (all the more so in the hyperstimulating, death-denying culture of modern America), mortality remains a permanent concern within the nonconscious dimensions of our minds. We always know we are going to die, but we do not always *know* we know; that is, we banish the thought from consciousness, we studiously avoid references to it, we forget it. This is why the discovery that you have a terminal illness can be such a painful and overwhelming experience: you are suddenly forced to confront consciously what the unconscious parts of your mind have been anxiously pondering from the earliest days of your childhood.

Dreams offer a vivid illustration of our lifelong awareness of death, giving voice to the unconscious fears, wishes, and desires that surround the brute fact of human finitude. Death is a remarkably prominent feature of historical and cross-cultural dream content, appearing in a wide variety of forms all over the world, and it remains a frequently recurring element in people's dreams today. Indeed, the unconscious nexus between dreaming and death is so strong that no theory of dreams, whether psychoanalytic, neuroscientific, or cognitive psychological, can be considered adequate if it fails to take this connection into account.

Seen from the perspective of the terminally ill, *all* dreams are pre-death dreams. *All* dreams, in more or less subtle ways, are searching meditations on the finitude of human life. Throughout our lives we are unconsciously preparing ourselves for death, and one of the functions of dreaming is precisely to create the meanings that will help us face the end with courage and understanding. We can learn much about this meaning-making process by exploring the basic themes and patterns in people's dreams across the life span, from childhood through old age. Knowing more about the fundamentals of human dream experience will provide a helpful context for our more focused discussion in later chapters on pre-death dream themes.

Across the Life Span

Dream researchers cannot say for sure when exactly children start dreaming. Some argue that the ability to dream depends on the sophisticated cognitive functions that do not develop until the ages of three or four, meaning that no true dreams are possible before then. Other researchers argue that rapid eye movement (REM) sleep—the stage of sleep during which most dreams happen—begins while a human fetus is still in the womb, and thus genuine dreaming *does* occur in the earliest periods of life even though children do not yet have the linguistic ability to describe their experiences.[9]

The mysteries of dreaming at the beginning of life thus foreshadow the mysteries of dreaming at the end of life.

What researchers do know is that many children experience frightening nightmares at a very early age, and many of these nightmares revolve around the threat of death. In the most primordial of these bad dreams, the child is thrust into a "chasing" scenario in which a malevolent antagonist is aggressively and relentlessly pursuing the young dreamer, who flees in terror. The sense of vulnerability and helplessness in such dreams is excruciating, and many people remember these intense experiences for the rest of their lives.

By the time of their school years most children have a clear understanding that all living creatures, including themselves, must eventually die. Many children, particularly those living close to nature in nonurban environments, also recognize that death is the precondition for new life. All creatures may die, but all creatures also have the ability to generate new life and thus to contribute to an ongoing process of life that extends beyond the death of the individual creature. When this realization develops in the mind of a child, the stage is set for the emergence of dreams in which death becomes a powerful metaphor for change, transformation, and creativity (all the more so in Christian communities, where the story of Jesus's resurrection teaches children a similar vision of death leading to new life).

Indeed, growing up itself involves a kind of dying, insofar as each new developmental gain puts a child's previous sense of selfhood farther and farther into the past. When a child dreams of death, then, it may not necessarily be about anyone's actual physical death, but rather about the metaphorical death of the child's own earlier personal identity. Thomas was a fourteen-year-old who suddenly began dreaming constantly about death—about people dying, animals slaughtered, dead bodies covering the ground, over and over again. Thomas's mother wondered what all these morbid death dreams could mean, since there had been no recent deaths in the family and Thomas's early teenage life was going pretty well. Indeed, his mother had noticed over the previous several weeks that Thomas had shown a noticeably greater interest in helping with household chores. He was keeping his room clean, doing the dishes, walking his dog twice a day, all without the usual reminders from his mother. She also found a paper in Thomas's room with a carefully written list of "resolutions" he had made for himself to get his life priorities in order. As Thomas's mother described this to Kelly, she said she experienced an "Aha!" moment of understanding about the dreams when she realized that Thomas was taking a major step into mature, independent, self-motivated adulthood—and in the process leaving a big part of his responsibility-free childhood behind. In a very real emotional sense, Thomas's childhood was "dying" and his new adult personality was being "born." The recurrent dreams of death and dying were accurate metaphorical expressions of what this growth process meant and felt like to Thomas.

While people frequently dream of the impending danger of death, they rarely dream of actually dying. The classic example is the falling dream, in which you tumble over a cliff or out of a plane, hurtling downward faster and faster toward certain death until you suddenly awaken, just a fraction of a second before hitting the ground. *Other* people may die in our dreams, but we ourselves usually find a way to break out of the dream before succumbing to whatever dire threat we may be facing. On those rare occasions when the dreamer does die within the dream, the physical sensations can be extraordinarily intense, with people describing feelings of their hearts exploding, or blood rushing through their heads, or a floating detachment from their bodies. These unusual qualities mark such dreams as particularly worthy of conscious reflection, with the strong possibility that a profound transformation is occurring in the dreamer's life.

Strange and unusual elements are often openings into creative insight and meaning making. Research based on collections of thousands of dreams suggests that most dreams do a surprisingly good job of recreating the ordinary conditions of our daily lives. The settings tend to be familiar, the characters known to us, the activities consistent with what we regularly do in waking life. Dreaming is by and large consistent with our interests and concerns in the regular waking world. This makes it all the more noticeable when certain dream elements jump out as being bizarre, improbable, and/or physically impossible. Some researchers argue that such fantastic elements in dream content are simply nonsense, evidence of the deficient cognitive abilities of the mind during sleep. Perhaps this is true for some percentage of dream bizarreness, but our experience is that many of the seemingly nonsensical oddities of dreaming turn out, on closer inspection, to be moments of spontaneous creative insight. What at first sight seems absurd and random can be recognized (in the "Aha!" moment) as surprisingly meaningful and relevant.

We will have much more to say about all this later in the book. For now we simply ask that you not dismiss "bizarre" dream elements out of hand, but hold open as a possibility the idea that the very strangest parts of people's dreams may serve as openings to new knowledge and wisdom.

To appreciate more fully what makes certain dreams strange and unusual, it helps to know what "average" dreaming is like. Enough research has been done over the past half century to provide a rough portrait of the most general features of dream experience, and this provides a useful backdrop for the evaluation of unusual types of dreams.[10] On average, men (particularly single men) dream much more about other men than about women. Their dreams contain twice as many male characters as female characters, while women tend to dream equally about male characters and female characters. Women dream more frequently of familiar people, men more of strangers. Indoor settings are more common for women, outdoor settings for men. Neither gender dreams very much about animals or about dead or imaginary characters (all of which occur more often in the dreams of children). Men's and women's dreams involve roughly equal proportions of friendly and aggressive interactions with other characters, though men's dreams have more physical aggression and more sexuality. Women's dreams have somewhat more emotional content, or at least their dream reports contain more explicit descriptions of their emotions. In both men's and women's dreams the emotions tend to be negative (sadness, anger, fear), and in both there are many more misfortunes (accidents, injuries, unforeseen difficulties, etc.) than good fortunes (miracles, lucky discoveries, etc.).

These empirical findings about dream content should not be taken as absolutely fixed or universal. Research in this area is still limited to a very small sample of the general population, and we already know that different cultural and psychological variables can have a huge influence on the specific details of people's dreams. Clearly, there is no single "right" or "normal" way to dream. But the value of learning about the broader patterns in dream content is this: knowing what is *ordinary* makes it easier to identify that which is truly *extra*ordinary. Comparing your dreams to the dreams of other people can bring out details you might not otherwise recognize. We will describe several examples of this in later chapters.

The study of dream journals kept by people for many decades has revealed that each individual's particular constellation of dream patterns is remarkably consistent over time. Each of us has our own set of signature dream themes that recur throughout our lives. From late adolescence through middle age, the basic proportions of dream content remain steady in terms of settings, scenarios, and characters. A striking example of this is a woman with the pseudonym "Dorothea" who provided researchers with her fifty-year dream journal (kept from 1912, when she was twenty-five, to 1963, when she was seventy-six). Study of her dreams found that six basic themes repeated with the same frequency throughout the fifty years, and at least one of these themes (eating or thinking of food, losing an object, being in a small room, being with her mother, going to the toilet, and being late for something) appeared in almost three-quarters of her dreams.[11] What this and other studies suggest is that dreams not only mirror the ups and downs of daily life, they also reflect the enduring qualities of our personality and the foundational concerns that shape our way of being in the world.

Significant changes in dream content come with old age, changes that stem from both the weakening physical abilities of many elderly people and their shrinking sphere of social interaction. Their dreams, not surprisingly, become preoccupied with themes of scarcity, confusion, loss of control, and loss of resources.[12] Typical dream themes of the elderly include difficulties cooking meals, toilets not working, misplacing familiar objects, and getting lost while driving a car. These recurrent negative dreams, combined with the deteriorating quality of sleep that many seniors experience, can lead to a diminished interest in dreaming and a consequent decrease in dream recall. What's the point of paying attention to dreams if all they do is remind you of depressing, insoluble problems you already know about?

We do not advocate reflection on dreams as a cure-all for everyone, but we want to emphasize strongly that an end-of-life diminution of dreaming *is not a necessary fate*—good sleep quality and a healthy relationship with the dreaming imagination are always possible. Sleep medicine has made enormous advances in recent years, and simple lifestyle practices (such as regular modest exercise, outdoor activity, and continued intellectual stimulation) have reliably beneficial effects on the length and restfulness of a night's sleep (for more on this, see William Dement's *The Promise of Sleep*[13]).

The dreams of the elderly, even if they come less frequently and have more disturbing content, are still valuable expressions of their creative imaginations, opening a window into the deepest realms of their psyches and offering helpful insights into the challenges of their waking lives. Caregivers play a crucial role in providing companionship for the elderly and the terminally ill as they try to make sense of their dreams, and one of our primary hopes in this book is to encourage caregivers in all contexts to include reflection on dreams as one element in their overall approach. If you can help others experience more restful sleep and a livelier awareness of their dreams, you will have done much for them, no matter what else ails them or how much time they have left to live.

Visitations

Let us widen our focus now and consider the pre-death dream experiences of people in other places and times. Here too we find many, many dreams that give people new existential insight into dying, death, and that which lies beyond death. This is particularly true in relation to the phenomenon of "visitation dreams." Striking, emotionally intense dreams in which a recently deceased loved one returns to provide guidance, reassurance, and/or warning have been reported throughout history in cultures all over the world. The remarkable cross-cultural frequency of visitation dreams is one of the strongest findings of anthropological dream research, and it points once again to the primal connection between dreaming and death.

But visitation dreams do not occur often. In fact, they seem to be quite rare, accounting for perhaps one percent of all dreams.[14] What makes visitation dreams so memorable is an unusual intensity and vividness that sharply distinguishes them from the majority of other dreaming experiences. People often speak of a visitation dream as feeling "realer than real," and when the dreamers awaken these electrifying feelings carry over into waking awareness, remaining surprisingly strong and easy to recollect many years later.

Here is a contemporary example that highlights the experiential power of visitation dreams, their role in the process of mourning, and the profound religious questions they raise.

Kim was a thirty-two-year-old teacher from Oregon who went with a group of friends to the hospital to visit their old college roommate Keith.[15] Keith had been stricken with cancer and was near death. Kim was overwhelmed by the horrifying sight of her good friend lying in the hospital's intensive care unit, heavily sedated and hooked up to a variety of life-support machines. From his hospital bed Keith was able to hear Kim and the others when they spoke to him, but he could respond to them only through a machine that beeped at each reaction. After they left the hospital Kim realized with a stab of regret that she had forgotten to hold Keith's hand one last time. She had been so overcome with emotion that she never physically touched him. A week later Keith died, and that night Kim had a dream:

I am lying in my bed when I see Keith at my bedside and feel the warmth of his skin as he slowly reaches for my hand. He stands close to me and holds my hand gently yet firmly for a long time. This feeling of his hand against mine is so real, too real to be a dream. In addition to the warmth of his flesh, I feel the firmness and thickness of his hand and the wrinkles that form on his palm and fingers as he holds my hand. (I almost opened my eyes to see if Keith were in fact standing by me, for I had never experienced in dreams feelings that felt so real.) Neither of us speak, nor is there any sound in the dream, and the atmosphere is that of tranquility.

When Kim awoke, the touch of Keith was still in her hand. She had not believed it was possible to have such intensely realistic physical sensations without actually holding another person's hand in her own. Kim was generally a skeptic regarding supernatural phenomena, and her work as a high school biology teacher gave her a strong appreciation for reason and science. Although she did not think her dream proved that ghosts or spirits really exist, she admitted that she had never had such an experience before, and she even hesitated to call it a dream because it was so uniquely realistic. She felt that somehow or other Keith really had come back, and he was trying to help ease her regrets about that last sad visit in the hospital. In the dream their positions are reversed—now Kim is the one lying motionless in bed, and Keith is standing beside her. Then he does what Kim wished *she* had done: he reaches for her hand and takes it in his own for a final, wordless goodbye.

It would be easy to explain away such dreams as mere Freudian wish-fulfillments, idle fantasies that offer a brief but comforting escape from the painful reality of a loved one's death. But such a dismissive view ignores the extraordinary and long-lasting emotional impact of such dreams and fails to appreciate their crucial role in the process of recentering oneself following a terrible loss. The enduring value of dreams like Kim's is precisely in the way they remind people of the ambiguous reality of death—the loved one is dead and physically gone, but something of the emotional relationship with that person remains alive and vividly present. Visitation dreams do not deny death so much as transcend it, providing experiential evidence of human connections that extend beyond the end of mortal life.

Given that so many people who experience visitation dreams insist on their hyperrealistic qualities, the question naturally arises as to whether or not these dreams are generated by *more* than the ordinary workings of the human brain-mind system and perhaps involve actual encounters with the souls of deceased loved ones. For a vast majority of the world's historical cultures, the answer to that question has been yes. For the aboriginal bands of Australia and the South Pacific, the tribal communities of Africa, the native peoples of North and South America, and the ancient civilizations of China, India, Egypt, and Greece, dreams have always been regarded as a primary means of maintaining contact with the spirits of the dead. Although these cultures have very different philosophical and spiritual worldviews, they share a fundamental belief that when we sleep, a part of ourselves (soul, spirit, ethereal self, etc.) is free to perceive other realities, travel to otherworldly realms, and gain important knowledge and wisdom. Death, in this perspective, is the final and permanent release of that part of ourselves, a sleep from which one never awakens, a dream that never ends.

This is why so many cultures have developed elaborate teachings to prepare a person for that final release. In ancient Egypt people who were about to die received a set of spells, prayers, and magical incantations (what we now collectively refer to as *The Egyptian Book of the Dead*). The spells were intended to provide the dying person with a practical guide for their journey to the afterlife, with warnings about potential obstacles, techniques to ward off evil spirits, and promises of assistance from the gods. Very similar to this is the Tibetan Buddhist text *Bardo Thödol,* generally translated as *The Tibetan Book of the Dead.* It too was (and still is) used to guide people in their passage from this life to the next, although the Tibetan Buddhist beliefs about this process are very different from the Egyptian. While the Egyptians sought to share a blissful afterlife with the gods in the Field of Reeds, Tibetan Buddhists believe that death leads to a fantastic realm of dream and vision, from which one goes either to rebirth as a new living (and suffering) creature, or to ultimate release and enlightenment. To help people achieve spiritual liberation and escape another painful cycle of bodily existence, the *Bardo Thödol* is traditionally read aloud to dying people so they can better recognize the strange new disembodied realities they will soon experience, and better resist the fearful desire to remain attached to the material world.

Different worldviews, but a similar approach to caregiving for the dying: ancient Egyptians, Tibetan Buddhists, and many other cultural traditions have developed powerful teachings to prepare people for that which lies beyond death, and paying close attention to dreams throughout one's life has always been an integral part of that preparation process. When the eighth-century B.C.E. Greek poet Hesiod wrote that death, sleep, and "the whole tribe of dreams" are brothers born of the goddess Night, he was expressing a fundamental human insight that dreaming is the closest thing to death we experience in this life.[16]

Near-Death Experiences

This is a good time to say something about the relationship between the subject of our book, pre-death dreams, and near-death experiences (NDEs). The writings of Raymond Moody, Kenneth Ring, Michael Sabom, and others have highlighted certain recurrent qualities and themes in the experiences of people whose respiration, heartbeat, and other vital signs temporarily stopped and who thus can be said to have "died" and come back to life. According to a sizable number of studies, NDE reports commonly include feelings of relaxation, peacefulness, and separation from one's body, along with visions of tunnels, bright lights, and numinous guiding figures. The intensity of NDEs often changes people's lives in radical ways, leading to less fear of human mortality and a greater spiritual appreciation for each present moment of this earthly life.

Controversy surrounds this subject, however, as some of the researchers have claimed their findings are scientific proof of life after death. This bold assertion has been rejected by skeptics who question the validity of NDE reports, which are impossible to verify and which are liable to all manner of revisions, modifications, and alterations so they fit better with the (often unconscious) expectations of the researchers. The people who have actually had NDEs, however, insist that they have truly gained a glimpse across the threshold of mortality, and that those skeptics who stubbornly refuse to believe their reports are clinging to an outmoded materialism that fears death rather than embracing it as a new mode of existence.

As interesting and important as this debate may be, our interests in this book will lead us in a very different direction. We do not want to prove anything about the afterlife, one way or the other. We do not want to argue over research methodologies, nor do we care to join in the hyperbole and name calling that unfortunately pervade the debate over NDEs. Our goals are much more limited, and more pragmatic. We are focusing on the here-and-now experience of the dying person, and we want to provide the dying person and his or her caregivers with good practical knowledge about the dreams, visions, and other revelatory phenomena that often occur in the final stage of life. The NDE literature offers several intriguing parallels to pre-death dreams, and we will mention some of them in the coming chapters. But, in our view, the differences between NDEs and pre-death dreams are equally significant. NDEs do not, by definition, happen to people who die, while the dreams we are discussing in this book do; the outcome of the experience is thus very different. NDEs occur very rarely, have little or no narrative content, and last but a brief moment. Pre-death dreams, by contrast, are a fairly regular occurrence among terminally ill people, are often filled with richly detailed narrative content, and can recur over the course of several nights.

Our view of NDEs and their relationship to pre-death dreams has been influenced by Carol Zaleski and her book *Otherworld Journeys: Accounts of Near-Death Experience in Medieval and Modern Times.* Zaleski explores the historical roots of NDEs and finds that what Moody, Ring, and other modern researchers are describing bears a striking resemblance to medieval Christian portrayals of the afterlife and what happens when a person dies. Without judging the reality of any of these experiences, Zaleski shows that modern NDE research is carrying on a visionary tradition that reaches back through many centuries of Western civilization. We greatly appreciate Zaleski's emphasis on historical self-awareness, her careful attention to the multiple dimensions of meaning (physical, psychological, cultural, mythic) in NDEs, and her openness to the religious energies they generate. To the extent that NDEs and pre-death dreams overlap, we want to bring these qualities of Zaleski's work to our more practically oriented discussion of caregiving for the dying.

Religion and/or Spirituality

Another overheated debate we wish to avoid concerns the precise distinction between *religion* and *spirituality*. Since our goal is to provide resources for dying people and their caregivers in the widest variety of contexts, we deliberately speak in terms that do not presuppose a particular faith, creed, or philosophy. At the same time, we have found as a matter of research and professional experience that a very high percentage of pre-death dreams call forth what are best described as religious and/or spiritual energies. We will continue to use these terms, then, even though there remains much scholarly disagreement about their proper denotation. We take them as roughly synonymous, both referring to the recognition and experience of powers that transcend our control and yet have a formative influence on, and discernible presence within, human life. Religion refers to a relatively more social appreciation of those powers, and spirituality to a relatively more individual engagement with them.

These are rough-and-ready definitions, but they will suffice for our purposes. The key point is that if we want to understand the dreams of the terminally ill, we must find some way to talk about the profoundly mysterious feelings, images, and energies that emerge within them. The world's religious traditions have developed languages to speak of such things, and we will continue to use those languages as long as they remain helpful.

With that in mind, let us consider two historical accounts of visitation dreams, one from the East and one from the West, and see how the religious and spiritual dimensions of meaning play out.

A Chinese Buddhist text from Yuan times (1279–1368 C.E.) tells of a lay believer named Wang Chiu-lien, who was a devout meditator seeking enlightenment in the Pure Land tradition. At night he dreamed of the Buddha, but always in the form of a sculpture, not as the living Buddha. He finally went to a monk and told him about these dreams. "This is easy to deal with," said the monk. "When you think of your late father, can you hold his usual comportment?"

Wang Chiu-lien answered yes, and the monk said, "Can you see him in your dreams in such a way that he is no different from when he was living?"

"There is no difference."

Satisfied, the monk said, "The Buddha in himself has no appearance. The appearance is manifested only in conformity with the way of things. From now on you should think of your late father as Amitabha [the Buddha]. Little by little, imagine that there are white streaks of light in between his brows, that his face is as of real gold, and that he sits on a lotus-flower. You can even imagine that his body grows larger and larger. Then your late father *is* himself the living Buddha."

Wang Chiu-lien applied this method according to the monk's instructions, so that whenever he dreamed of his father he told himself, "This is the Buddha." In time, he dreamed that his father led him to sit on the lotus, where he explained to his son the essence of the Buddhist teachings.[17]

This story makes explicit and deliberate what is usually implicit and spontaneous in visitation dreams: the valuable role of those who have died in guiding the dreamer toward a closer relationship with religious powers and spiritual truths. The point of the monk's instructions to Wang Chiu-lien is to encourage him to make an intentional effort to deepen his dreaming engagement with his deceased father as a means of connecting more fully with those powers that transcend ordinary mortal life. This is exactly what religious traditions at their best try to do, namely, to help people cultivate their sense of creative engagement with forces greater than themselves. For all the reasons we have been discussing, visitation dreams have always been a phenomenon of great religious interest, and Buddhism is by no means the only tradition to teach methods of exploring dreams with greater spiritual intentionality. The Native American vision quest, the shamanic journeys of Siberian shamans, the ecstatic trances of African healers, the healing sanctuaries of the Greek god Asclepius, these and many other dream incubation practices can be found in the world's religions, and they all share the goal of provoking a closer interaction between the dreamers and transcendent spiritual powers. The monk's comment that the Buddha's appearance in human awareness is never pure but always "manifested in conformity with the way of things" underscores the variability of people's conceptualizations of these powers. Your dream of the divine is not necessarily the same as other people's dreams, but you can be sure that your dream is true, relevant, and appropriate for *you* and your current life situation.

A second story, from the early Christian context, also highlights the personal specificity of dreaming and the revelatory insights about death that can be gained from close attention to one's dreams. St. Augustine of Hippo (d. 430 C.E.), one of the Christian tradition's most influential theologians, once received a letter from a friend who asked his opinion about dreams and the soul's existence after death. Augustine replied by describing the dream experience of a man he knew named Gennadius. Gennadius had also been wondering about the afterlife, when he had a dream in which a strange young man showed Gennadius a beautiful city filled with the music of hymns being sung to the saints. The next night Gennadius had a second dream in which the young man reappeared and directly asked Gennadius whether it was in sleep or when awake that he had seen the city. Gennadius answered, "In sleep."

The young man then said, "You remember it well: it is true that you saw these things in sleep, but I would have you know that even now you are seeing in sleep." Hearing this, Gennadius was persuaded of its truth, and in reply declared that he believed it. Then the young man went on to ask, "Where is your body now?"

Gennadius answered, "In my bed."

"Do you know," the youth asked, "that the eyes in this body of yours are now bound and closed, and at rest, and that with these eyes you are seeing nothing?"

"I know it," Gennadius answered.

"What, then," the young man continued, "are the eyes with which you see me?" Unable to discover what to answer to this, Gennadius fell silent.

In this moment of uncertainty and paradox, the youth finally revealed to Gennadius the deeper truth of his experience. "As while you are asleep and lying on your bed these eyes of your body are now unemployed and doing nothing, and yet you have eyes with which you behold me, and enjoy this vision, so, after your death, while your bodily eyes shall be wholly inactive, there shall be in you a life by which you shall still live, and a faculty of perception by which you shall still perceive. Beware, therefore, after this of harboring doubts as to whether the life of man shall continue after death." Augustine ends his recounting of the story by asking, "By whom was Gennadius taught this but by the merciful, providential care of God?"[18]

To be sure, the lesson that Augustine draws from Gennadius's experience is very different from the lesson taught to Wang Chiu-lien by the Buddhist monk. This is an important point—*all dreams do not point to a single truth, reality, or divine power.* We disagree with claims that all religious and mystical traditions lead to the same realization of pure consciousness, peak experience, absolute unitary being, or any other monolithic, one-size-fits-all state of mind. At least in the realm of dreaming, the revelatory experience is so deeply rooted in the individual's personal life history and cultural context that it makes no sense to try and extract a "universal core" from it. Gennadius and Wang Chiu-lien both had dreams of great spiritual power, but not necessarily of the *same* power. Their dreams spoke to where each of them was at that moment, in the rich symbolic language of their different religious traditions, and they each received valuable (though different) insights into the nature of the soul, in this life and beyond.

Another feature to note in Gennadius's dream is the quality of self-awareness within the dream state itself, often referred to as dream lucidity. Augustine's account is one of the earliest mentions of lucid dreaming in the Western tradition. In the Upanishads of ancient India (sixth century B.C.E.), self-awareness within dreaming is mentioned and affirmed as a state of consciousness that opens the way to new vistas of existential knowledge. Tibetan Buddhists have developed meditation practices that aim, in coordination with the *Bardo Thödol,* to cultivate dream lucidity as a way of preparing for what will happen after death. In contemporary American society only a small percentage of people report being self-aware in their dreams, and psychological researchers are divided about what, if anything, lucid dreaming means in terms of brain-mind functioning.

Once again, there is no one right path in the world of dreaming. Some people regularly experience lucid dreams and find them to be tremendous sources of spiritual discovery. Other people never have a lucid dream with that kind of impact, but still have incredibly powerful dreams that transform their understanding of themselves and the world. What happened to Gennadius—a full-blown state of self-awareness, allowing for profound reflection on the true nature of the soul—is one of the many strange potentials of dreaming, a rare but striking aberration from ordinary dreaming that leads to a deeper spiritual sensitivity. The pre-death dreams we discuss in this book often involve unusual shifts, expansions, and intensifications of self-awareness, and we recommend paying particular attention to them as possible indicators of a new development in the dreamer's preparation for dying.

A final point about Augustine's description of Gennadius's dream: we have here a major Christian theologian (some would say the most decisive and authoritative figure in the early church) who is explicitly saying that at least some dreams come from God. This is important to remember because many Christians today are taught to avoid dreams as potentially sinful temptations sent by the Devil. While it is true that several passages from the Bible emphasize the ephemerality of dreams and their potential to deceive people, many other passages highlight the positive power of dreams to provide divine guidance, reassurance, and warning.[19] Indeed, the Bible never once mentions demons or the Devil as tempting people in their dreams. That belief is a later addition to the Christian tradition, and it has unfortunately led to an automatic hostility toward dreaming among several Christian communities (particularly those who identify themselves as religious conservatives or fundamentalists).

We respectfully disagree with that theological perspective.

We believe a careful reading of the Bible does not support the beliefs that God's faithful should ignore dreams and that dream interpretation is a sin. If there is any general message about dreams to be drawn from the Bible, it is this: dreams are one of the ways that God's spirit enters people's lives. Although a dream may initially appear strange or frightening, a person who has faith, a discerning judgment, and perhaps the help of an experienced interpreter, can eventually grasp its meaning. St. Augustine understood this all the way back in 400 C.E., and many contemporary Christians today do as well. The writings of Morton Kelsey, John Sanford, Louis Savary and Patricia Berne, Wallace and Jean Clift, James Hall, Jeremy Taylor, and numerous others testify to the continuing vitality of dreaming and dream interpretation in the contemporary Christian tradition.[20]

Your Life as a Dreamer

The close connection between sleep, dreaming, and death is the stuff of myth and mysticism. According to the world's religious traditions, through this doorway lie otherworldly realms of divine mystery, where liberated souls make wonderful journeys of discovery and revelation.

On a more personal scale, the sleep-dreaming-death nexus provides each of us with a valuable source of insight into our own individual feelings, beliefs, hopes, and desires surrounding the inevitability of death. This is our first major piece of practical advice: reflect back over your life as a dreamer— think of your most memorable dreams, the dreams that made you happy, that scared you, that puzzled and mystified you. Consider those dreams in terms of the full arc of your life. People who are terminally ill have a precious opportunity to take some time to reflect on their lives as a narrative whole, as a grand story with a beginning, middle, and end. Your dreams have always been a kind of running commentary on that story, mirroring your life's experiences and weaving them into a meaningful reality, and now at the end of life you are in a position to see that process from a new perspective. We suggest you give special attention to the kinds of dreams we have discussed in this chapter—dreams relating to death, visitation dreams, lucid dreams, and unusually "bizarre" dreams —as particularly potent sources of personal insight and self-understanding.

It is less important to *interpret* such dreams than simply to *be with them*. Intellectual analysis has its place, and in the next chapter we will describe some methods to use in reflecting on dreams and discerning their different levels of meaning. But none of that should be taken as a substitute for the deeper process that unfolds as you allow your dreams a welcome place in waking awareness. That's where the transformational effect of dreaming really begins.

CHAPTER 2

THE NATURE AND
MEANING OF DREAMS

Basic Principles

In this chapter we will go over a few basic principles that can help you in your efforts to discern meaning in dreams. We will discuss the strange language used by dreams to express themselves, the metaphorical qualities of their meaning, their function in anticipating the future, and the process we use for interpreting a particular dream. If you already feel comfortable with your dreamwork skills, and/or if you want to start reading immediately about some actual reports of people's pre-death dream experiences, feel free to skip ahead to Chapter 3.

The Strange Language of Dreaming

"If dreams are so valuable and beneficial for our lives, why are they so hard to understand? Why don't they just say what they mean in clear, easily comprehensible language?"

That's a question people ask us in one form or another almost every time we talk about dreams. Sometimes the question is posed in more skeptical terms, as a challenge to the very idea that dreams are meaningful at all. Other times the question reflects a person's sincere desire to learn from his or her dreams, a desire that is frustrated by the baffling imagery and inexplicable oddities that pervade the dream world. Either way, the issue is a real one, and it needs to be addressed before we can confidently move ahead to explore the potential meanings of pre-death dreams. How can you figure out what a dream means, and how can you ever be sure you aren't simply fooling yourself by reading preexisting meanings *into* the dream?

Our approach is to think of dream interpretation as comparable to visiting a foreign country. If you were to travel to a faraway land, you would find people conversing and carrying on their lives using their own language. Initially you might not understand what the people were saying, and you would probably feel some degree of confusion and dislocation. As uncomfortable as that might feel, however, you would not get very far if you waited for all of them to learn *your* language, just to make life easier for you. If you really wanted to learn about them, you would have to make the effort to understand *their* language and all the other forms of communication native to that community. This would take time, patience, and a willingness to plunge forward despite a constant sense of uncertainty. But the effort would bear fruit—gradually you would build up enough experience that you could speak the language, and this would enable you to join in an ongoing conversation with the people. What had initially sounded like pure gibberish could now be appreciated as meaningful and creative communication.

This is the way it is with dreams. They often seem bizarre, absurd, and incomprehensible at first, but patient reflection usually leads to the discernment of genuine meaning and intelligence emerging within them.

Now imagine, if you will, that two travel companions come along to join you, Sigmund Freud and Carl Jung. Each has his own attitude toward learning about the people and their language.

The ever-suspicious Freud would say, "These foreigners are

trying to *hide* their ideas from me, using this strange language as a deceptive façade to mislead me. But I know how to break down that façade, uncover the dark repressed meanings, and translate them into proper German."

The more mystically inclined Jung would reply, "No, no, the people are simply using a regional variant of the natural language of the psyche, which is ultimately the same for all people in all places and times. If we can teach ourselves that language, we will have the universal key to all religion and mythology."

Neither of these approaches, taken by itself, offers totally trustworthy guidance in the interpretation of dreams. We share Freud's concern that dream interpretation is often clouded by emotional resistance to the unsettling insights and painful self-revelations that regularly emerge in dreams. However, we disagree with Freud when he claims that dreaming is a defensive, regressive process that cunningly seeks to elude conscious attention. We agree with Jung that dreams are hard to understand not because they are intentionally deceptive, but because they are generated by a state of mind very different from waking awareness. Jung has a much greater appreciation than Freud does for the transformative power of dreaming, and our approach in this book is deeply influenced by Jung's teachings about dreaming as a source of psychospiritual growth. Still, we do not follow him on all points, and we are particularly critical of Jung's tendency to assert the absolute universality of his archetypal symbols. Cross-cultural patterns in dreaming certainly exist, and Jung is a good guide to understanding them. But claiming that such patterns are permanent fixtures of the mind is excessive and unnecessary. Most problematically, a universalistic perspective can blind us to what is unique, singular, and idiosyncratic in a dream. A Jungian effort to uncover a dream's archetypal symbolism is, in this regard, the same as a Freudian effort to break down a dream's manifest façade to find its latent wish—both are reductive practices that discourage any appreciation for the distinct creative power of *this particular dream.*

As we have already mentioned, we favor an approach to dream interpretation that balances cross-cultural patterns with personal life context. In this chapter we will describe our approach in more detail, focusing on the metaphorical language of dreaming and the practical methods that can be used to develop a greater understanding of that language. We will also discuss one of the principal functions of dreaming as it relates to pre-death dreams—the function of preparing us for future challenges.

Metaphors We Live By, and Die By

Metaphors are often thought of as mere literary embellishments, as poetic expressions that decorate language and enhance rhetorical persuasion. But recent studies by George Lakoff, Mark Johnson, and other linguists have shown that *metaphorical thinking is in fact the conceptual foundation of all our experiences in the world.* Metaphors pervade our thought, language, and reasoning, not just in art and poetry but in our ordinary, everyday lives—and not just in waking, but in dreaming as well.

The essence of metaphor is "understanding one kind of thing in terms of another."[21] We use what we *know* to help us understand what we *don't* know. This comes naturally to us—human brains have evolved a vast capacity for associating different ideas with each other as a means to greater knowledge and adaptive creativity. Metaphorical thinking is in many ways the defining trait of our species, giving us tremendous flexibility in creative problem solving when faced with novel circumstances. Metaphors are most obviously at work in cases where we try to understand experiences that are strange and intangible by using our knowledge of other things that are more concrete and clear. For example, love is an experience that defies easy description, so we frequently resort to metaphors of physical force to talk about it. We speak of the "electricity" between people, feeling "sparks," "gravitating" toward someone, "falling" in love, getting "hot," and so forth. We use our more tangible experiences with physical force as metaphorical maps to help us understand the less tangible experience of love.

More to the point here, Lakoff and Turner discuss the metaphorical dimensions of our understanding of death. In the Preface to *More than Cool Reason: A Field Guide to Poetic Metaphor,* they describe the multiple metaphors used to think about life and death. Since these existential themes are so mysterious and all-encompassing, people employ many different metaphors in the effort to make sense of them. A particularly widespread general metaphor in this regard is *life is a journey.* A journey is a relatively tangible and easily comprehended experience, and it offers a wealth of metaphorical correspondences that illuminate qualities of human life as a whole. These correspondences include:

- The person leading a life is a traveler.
- His or her purposes are destinations.
- The means for achieving purposes are routes.
- Difficulties in life are impediments to travel (e.g. , road blocks).
- Counselors are guides.
- Progress is the distance traveled.
- Things you gauge your progress by are landmarks.
- Choices in life are crossroads.
- Material resources and talents are provisions.

The mapping of aspects of a journey onto aspects of the nature of life can be further extended to help in the comprehension of death. Death can be understood as the end of life's journey, as a departure, as a trip to one's final destination.

And to the extent that life is also metaphorically conceived as moving upward, into light, waking, and the day, death becomes a going downward into darkness, into sleep, and into the night.

No metaphor has an absolutely fixed meaning—the natural genius of the human imagination is its ability to create novel extensions of preexisting ideas. This is precisely what happens so often in dreaming, when the unconscious dimensions of the mind spin waking metaphors into fanciful tapestries of image, space, and mood. Lakoff puts it very succinctly: "Dreams are not just the weird and meaningless product of random neural firings but rather the natural way by which emotionally charged fears, desires, and descriptions are expressed."[22] When we look at the dreams that come before death, we find the metaphor-generating system of the mind working with extraordinary intensity to make sense of something that is, by its very nature, outside the realm of lived experience. This makes pre-death dreams both unusually challenging to understand and potentially profound in their revelatory insight.

Knowing something about metaphorical thinking is necessary in making proper use of dream symbol dictionaries. Almost everyone involved in the study of dreams scorns these formulaic little books as the worst of crude interpretation-by-the-numbers. And yet, almost everyone makes use of the same common associations of certain dream images with certain meanings. The reason for this is that we are all working with cultural storehouses of metaphor that can be used with greater or lesser degrees of sophistication and flexibility. This is why, for example, a dream dictionary can say an image of a package could mean "hidden or wrapped away emotions/resources."[23] Such an association has intuitive plausibility because of our familiarity with the common metaphor of emotions as entities or substances within a person (for example, "I'm filled with joy" or "He's steaming mad"). Likewise with a dream of milk and the idea that "feeding/giving another [person] milk may symbolize giving basic life energy, nurturing at an elemental/primal level."[24] This makes sense because of what we know of mother's milk as the original form of nourishment.

Still, you can't be certain these metaphorical connections actually apply to a given person's dream. You can only be sure of that if you take into account the dreamer's personal and cultural life situation. A dream of a tidal wave might mean one thing to a person living in Hawaii, another to a person living in Kansas, another to a parent with a newborn, and still another to someone who lost a friend in a boating accident. We suggest a cautious reliance on symbol dictionaries as repositories of metaphorical possibility, as one means of stimulating new thought about what may be emerging in a dream. Ultimately, though, only the dreamer can know whether or not a particular interpretation is true to his or her experience.

The Anticipatory Function

So far we have been speaking about the "how" of dream expression, the metaphorical language by which dreams articulate themselves in our imaginations. The question to consider now is the "what" of dreaming. What are the denizens of this strange land talking about? What are they trying to achieve in their nightly conversations? Why should we pay any attention to them and their seemingly bizarre activities?

These questions lead us to research on the functions of dreaming. This is another academic minefield, and here again we do not want to become caught in the scholarly crossfire between rival theorists. Freud's claim that dreaming serves the twin functions of covert wish-fulfillment and sleep preservation has not fared well in light of recent scientific research, though some psychoanalytic thinkers continue to use his model. Other theories claim that dreaming helps to process new information, strengthen our memory, respond adaptively to environmental dangers, keep our emotional balance, and maintain the psychological integrity of the self.[25] These claims all have evidence to support them, but none of them has achieved anything close to consensus agreement among researchers. A hundred years after Freud, we are realizing that dreaming is far more complex and multifaceted than he ever imagined. The more we learn, the more we discover about the amazing diversity of dream types, functions, and meanings.

Our interest in pre-death dreams leads us to focus our attention on one particular dimension of dream function. Dreams frequently anticipate the future, preparing the dreamer for possible challenges, dangers, and opportunities in waking life. This is not necessarily the only or the best function of dreaming, but it is one that we can understand in relatively straightforward terms, and it is directly relevant to the powerful experiential impact of pre-death dreams. We believe a key function of these dreams is to *look ahead*, to envision what lies before one in the journey of life, to prepare oneself physically, emotionally, and spiritually for the mysterious passage from this world to whatever comes next.

The anticipatory function both is and is not related to the nearly universal belief in the prophetic or precognitive powers of dreaming. People throughout history have reported dreams that seemed to accurately foretell future events, most frequently of a disastrous nature, like accidents, illnesses, and unexpected deaths. Sometimes these dreams can be explained as mere coincidences. For example, enough people dream about car crashes that eventually one day someone who dreamed of a car crash the night before will actually have one in the waking world. That's not prophecy, that's just the law of averages. Some reports of precognitive dreaming may even be fabricated or at least unconsciously embellished by people who wish for the magical power to see into the future. Research in this area is notoriously difficult to conduct, and a healthy skepticism should be maintained when considering reports of predictive dreams.

Still, a growing body of evidence is supporting the idea that among its many functions, dreaming does indeed look toward the future, helping people respond to the most difficult and troubling emotional problems of their daily lives. An early recognition of this comes in Jung's notion of "the prospective function" of dreams. Jung is better known (and more frequently criticized) for his claim that dreaming serves a "compensatory" function, by which the excesses of waking consciousness are balanced by corrective dreams aiming to produce greater psychological wholeness. The prospective function is different, highlighting the way certain dreams bring together various perceptions, thoughts, memories, and feelings in a way that helps envision possible aspects of the dreamer's future. Jung says that in such dreams we find

> An anticipation in the unconscious of future conscious achievements, something like a preliminary exercise or sketch, or a plan roughed out in advance. Its symbolic content sometimes outlines the solution of a conflict.... The occurrence of prospective dreams cannot be denied. It would be wrong to call them prophetic, because at bottom they are no more prophetic than a medical diagnosis or a weather forecast. They are merely an anticipatory combination of probabilities which may coincide with the actual behavior of things but need not necessarily agree in every detail. Only in the latter case can we speak of "prophecy." That the prospective function of dreams is sometimes greatly superior to the combinations we can consciously foresee is not surprising, since a dream results from the fusion of thoughts and feelings which consciousness has not registered because of their feeble accentuation. In addition,

dreams can rely on subliminal memory traces that are no longer able to influence consciousness effectively. With regard to prognosis, therefore, dreams are often in a much more favorable position than consciousness.[26]

Other researchers have used different terms to describe the anticipatory function. Psychoanalysts Thomas French and Erika Fromm have spoken of dreams as addressing the "focal conflicts" of people's lives, in other words, those conflicts that are most pressing and yet most difficult to resolve. Drawing on their extensive clinical experience, French and Fromm argue that dreams are "groping to understand problems that cannot yet be adequately grasped" and striving toward possible solutions that may be achieved in the future.[27] Sleep laboratory researcher Rosalind Cartwright's book *Crisis Dreaming* describes numerous dreams that anticipate in various ways people's upcoming encounters with childbirth, illness, and death, all of which provide evidence for an unconscious rehearsal function: "Dreams review the experiences that give rise to strong feelings and match them to related images from the past. They enable us to revise our pictures of our present selves and to rehearse our responses to future challenges."[28]

Neuroscientist J. Allan Hobson suggests that REM sleep and dreaming may function to rehearse basic motor programs (especially the fight-or-flight system and the orienting response): "The motor programs in the brain are never more active than during REM sleep, [helping] to prevent their decay from disuse, to rehearse for their future actions when called on during waking, and to embed themselves in a rich matrix of meaning."[29] This function of exercising basic motor programs extends to extremely positive dreams like those of flying, as Hobson says "our ecstatic dreams equip us for the elation and joy of life."[30] And Antti Revonsuo, a neuroscientist from Finland, has recently argued that dreaming works to simulate potential dangers in our environment, with the beneficial result that we are better prepared to face such threats when they actually arise in waking life. As evidence of what he calls "the threat simulation function," Revonsuo points to the vivid realism of dreaming, its frequent portrayal of frightening threats, and its tendency to be triggered into heightened activation by experiences of physical danger.[31]

We can summarize all these ideas by saying that *in dreams we wonder about the future.* In our dreams we anticipate the future, envision it, ponder it, play with it, worry about it, rehearse it. Dreams are especially engaged with aspects of the future that have strong emotional meaning for us, pertaining to particularly troubling, unsettling, and/or exciting prospects. When we go to sleep our imaginations are released from the constraints of external perception, allowing a freer exploration of potential developments in times to come. We can take different perspectives on our lives, consider alternative possibilities, explore hypothetical scenarios. We can see what it would feel like if we did this, or said that, or went there—the world of dreaming is the ultimate testing ground where anything can be tried, practiced, or rehearsed.

Examples of anticipatory dreams can be drawn from every stage of life. Among young children, the frequency of chasing nightmares helps to stimulate greater vigilance toward real threats in the waking world. Having a terrifying, highly realistic dream of being attacked by a wild animal may be emotionally distressing, but it certainly makes a child more alert to the same thing happening in waking life, and that's very beneficial in terms of promoting a child's chances for survival. Older children often have anticipatory dreams in relation to starting a new school, going away to camp, or moving to a different neighborhood. Any time we face a major change in our lives, our dreaming imaginations go to work preparing us for what might happen and how we can best respond.

In adolescence, boys and girls regularly report sexual dreams before they have actually had any sexual experience.

Such dreams can be understood as "priming the pumps," getting the reproductive system up and running so it will be ready for action whenever the opportunity arises in the waking world. Young women periodically dream of being pregnant, sometimes with joyful ecstasy at the feeling of a new life growing within them, sometimes with dread at being a parent too soon. When women do become pregnant, their dreams regularly envision what the labor and delivery will feel like and how the baby will appear and behave once it's born. (In Korea, pre-birth dreams, or *taemong,* are avidly sought as prophetic indicators of the child's future personality and fortune.) After a child is born, both mothers and fathers are subject to frightening dreams in which the child is lost, injured, or ill; just like chasing nightmares in childhood, these parenting anxiety dreams have the positive effect of heightening vigilance toward possible threats in the environment, and in evolutionary terms this is promoting our ultimate biological goal of reproducing and nurturing to maturity a new generation of our species.

Later in life we continue to wonder about the future in our dreams, especially when we are confronted with situations that are strange, frightening, and beyond our ordinary sphere of control. An unfortunate example of this has appeared in recent years with the advent of "terrorist nightmares." Following the September 11, 2001, attack on the World Trade Center in New York and the Pentagon in Washington, D.C., people all across the United States have been experiencing dreams in which they find themselves suddenly in the midst of a new terrorist attack—the plane they're on is taken over by hijackers, or their hometown is struck by missiles and bombs, or they find themselves fighting in a confusing war. These dreams are not necessarily predictions of specific future events, but rather fear-driven anticipations of what would happen, what it would *feel* like, if the dreamer actually found him- or herself in the midst of a terrorist attack. In research Kelly did on the impact of September 11th on dreams, he heard this dream from a twenty-one-year-old female college student: "I was a passenger on an airplane and I was prepared in the event that there were hijackers on the plane. I made sure I had an aisle seat so that if there were terrorists on the plane I would be able to attack them." Besides being a worrisome sign of the times, this young woman's experience is a perfect example of the anticipatory function of dreaming. The dream responds to a perceived threat in the waking world with an imagined rehearsal of how she could most effectively act if that threat actually came to pass.

Seen in this light, pre-death dreams can be recognized as a final opportunity for the anticipatory function to serve its purpose. The dreaming imagination is naturally drawn to envision this greatest of transformations, and as the end of life approaches people's dreams focus increasingly on the mysterious future that awaits them. As with other prospective dreams, those that come prior to death can be either frightening or joyful, but in almost all cases the dreams have the effect of expanding, enhancing, and enriching people's awareness of themselves and the world.

New Dreams: What You Can Learn from Them

In the first chapter we asked you to recall the most memorable dreams of your life, allowing them to enter conscious awareness once again. Now we suggest you begin listening for new dreams, dreams that come in response to your new (or renewed) interest in this realm of your life. People's dream recall regularly increases as a consequence of reading a book, taking a class, or seeing something on television about dreams—dreaming is surprisingly responsive to waking attention, and simply *thinking* a bit more about dreams is usually all it takes to remember more of them. We recommend you write your dreams in a notebook, or describe the dreams to someone else who can write them down for you. Not only does this help clarify the dream in your memory, it also allows you to track recurrent images and themes that appear in your dreams over time. Nothing can beat a dream journal as a source of long-term personal insight and self-revelation.

A word of caution, though: dream recall cannot be forced, so try not to set unreasonable expectations for how many dreams you think you should be remembering. If sleep laboratory research is right in concluding that our minds are active in some form or another all through the night, then all of us are forgetting the vast majority of dreams. Be content with those dreams you do remember, focus on learning as much as you can from them, and don't worry about all the ones you're inevitably forgetting. What matters isn't the quantity of dreams you recall, but the quality of your reflections on the ones that remain in your memory.

When telling or writing out your dreams, try using the present rather than the past tense. This helps bring the dream back to life, reviving its immediate presence in your awareness. Compare "I went downstairs and saw a man who was pointing a gun at me" to "I go downstairs and see a man who is pointing a gun at me." If you read the two sentences aloud, you can hear the greater liveliness of the latter version. Also, try describing the dream in as much detail as possible, including even those elements that seem trivial or unimportant. It is the nature of dreams that sometimes seemingly minor details turn out to express valuable meanings that enrich one's overall understanding.

So what can you do once you've shared and/or written out your dreams? When people begin the process of trying to interpret a dream, they often have one of two different reactions. The first is silence and an uncomfortable and vaguely threatening sense of confusion: "Hmm, I have absolutely *no* idea what this dream could mean." The second reaction, by contrast, is an overwhelming urge to *talk*, to give instant voice to all the ideas and insights that come rushing to mind. Both reactions are understandable, but both have the effect of impeding the process of interpretation. The first response exaggerates the difficulty of discerning the dream's meanings, and the second exaggerates the speed and simplicity of grasping those meanings. In both cases the interpretive process is short-circuited before it even begins.

The easiest way to begin exploring a dream is to ask questions of *specification*. This means going through each of the dream's elements and asking why, out of all the infinite possibilities available, does this dream portray *these* particular details. Remember, dreams have nearly infinite creativity at their disposal—dreams can set us in any place, with anyone, doing anything. The question to ask is, why does the dream choose to present just *this* place, *these* characters, and *these* activities? Take as an example a dream of seeing a boyfriend from high school riding in a blue car through a jungle. Questions of specification would be, what are the main personality characteristics of that boyfriend? How was your relationship with him different from your relationship with other boyfriends? How would the dream be different if instead of him, your mother was in the car? Or your father, or a sibling, or your best friend? Why, of all the people who could have been presented in this dream, did this particular boyfriend appear? What about the blue car—how would the dream be different if it were white, or red, or silver? How is a car different from, say, riding a bus, a bicycle, a train? What are the special qualities of a jungle as compared to a city street, or a garden, or a desert?

When these kinds of questions are asked of a dream, the answers initially come in the form of a stream of memories, associations, and connections between the dream and various waking-life thoughts and experiences. At the outset it is wise to allow this stream of ideas to flow as freely as possible, without prematurely settling on one or another association as "the meaning" of the dream. It's easy to stop the interpretation right here, after some initial connections have been made between elements of the dream and waking-life memories. People are often tempted at this stage to say, "Oh, so *that's* what the dream is about, now I understand." To end the interpretation here, however, leaves much of the dream's value unrealized. Questions of specification can reveal a great deal of essential information about where the dream has come from, but they do not give much insight into where the dream is *going*. To learn more about where the dream might be leading the dreamer, to discover what new directions for growth and development are being revealed, a different set of questions is needed. Four questions are especially useful in this regard.

First, what is the most vivid element in the dream, the point of greatest energy, intensity, and vitality? This element may be an especially vivid and radiant character, a surprisingly strong physical sensation, a brightly colored object, or a strikingly beautiful setting. Whatever it is, focusing your attention on this point (or points—there may be more than one area of heightened vitality) is important because this is a place where the dreaming imagination has generated something special and unusual, something that stands out from everything else in the dream. By inviting this extraordinary dream element into consciousness and playfully pondering its unique qualities and attributes, a wealth of new insights into the dream as a whole can be discovered.

Second, are there any abrupt shifts or changes in the setting, the characters, or the narrative of the dream? These changes are usually signaled by the words "suddenly" or "just then"—"I am in my backyard gardening, when suddenly a leprechaun appears before me...." "Just then the scene shifts, and I'm back in high school...." It is helpful to focus special attention on these sudden shifts because in most cases, these are points where the dreaming imagination is bringing something *new* into the dream. A moment of abrupt change is a moment when novel possibilities are coming into the dreamer's awareness, when new connections are being made across different aspects of daily life, when the dreamer is confronting aspects of reality that he or she may never have consciously noticed or thought about before.

Third, what is the weirdest, most bizarre, most "counterfactual" element in the dream? Most dreams portray events that either have actually happened, or could conceivably happen in the normal daily life of the dreamer. Some dreams, however, have elements that are utterly strange and bizarre, elements that could not possibly be found in regular waking life. If your dream has one or more elements that sharply deviate from the normal realities of your life, it is worth reflecting carefully on what strange new perspectives the counterfactual element might be conveying to your conscious awareness.

Fourth, are there any notable patterns of symmetry and contrast in the dream? A variety of basic binary oppositions regularly appear in people's dreams—fundamental distinctions between male and female, child and adult, kin and non-kin, profane and sacred, good and evil, hot and cold, dry and wet, day and night, up and down, back and front, left and right, white and black, dead and alive, light and dark, one and many, and so on. Close analysis of a dream usually shows that it has been formed out of a surprisingly complex pattern of symmetries and contrasts between these dyadic elements. Identifying this pattern can help you recognize unexpected dimensions of meaning. Perhaps most importantly, reflecting on the dream's structural elements can open up new perspectives on how to overcome painful conflicts between opposing elements in your current life.

Spending some time with these four questions puts you in a good position to explore and evaluate the dream's roots in your past experiences. Particularly when a person is going through a time of serious change or crisis, dreams come that connect the current life situation to the broader context of the individual's life. For example, a person contemplating divorce may have dreams involving past romantic relationships, past experiences of loss and mourning, and/or past experiences of being single and unattached. Such dreams respond to present-day difficulties by recalling similar situations from earlier times of life (sometimes all the way back to childhood, as Freud realized), bringing to conscious awareness feelings and memories that can help the dreamer deal better with the current life challenges.

As we have seen, dreams do not only look backward into the dreamer's past, they also look forward into the future, into the potentials and possibilities on the far horizons of the dreamer's life. Dreams may not be able to help you pick winning lottery numbers or predict future prices on the stock market, but they definitely have the power to anticipate future contingencies and rehearse your responses to them. Thus, a vital element in any effort to interpret a dream is the question, what new possibilities for the future are revealed in this dream? Continuing with the example of a person contemplating divorce, does the dream envision what life might be like after a divorce? Does it imagine any new ways in which the relationship might be saved? Does it point to ways in which the dreamer will be changed and transformed whether or not the divorce actually happens?

Asking these kinds of future-oriented questions does not yield simple, clear-cut answers. What comes instead is a widening of perception, a liberation from previous conceptual boundaries, an opening of new forms of awareness, insight, and sensitivity. Particularly when a person is facing the end of his or her life, when the future might seem hopeless and no escape from despair seems possible, powerful dreams often come to revive the individual's capacity to think freely and creatively about the future. The value of these dreams is not only their specific content (though it may be profound) but also the way they show that the dreamer's basic ability to hope is still alive.

Dreams rarely if ever have one single, unambiguous meaning. On the contrary, most dreams have multiple dimensions of meaning, some that emerge right away and others that take much longer to reach conscious awareness. As a consequence, there is no definite rule about when an interpretation of a dream is finished. You are left to decide for yourself at what point you should stop, once you have discerned those meanings that seem most relevant to your current life situation. Often there comes a moment when the interpretation reaches a natural ending point, when you sense the time has come to bring your reflections to a close.

But before you do so, take a moment to consider this. The single greatest obstacle to understanding dreams comes in the form of *resistance*—the discomfort and reluctance people feel when anxiety-provoking energies from a dream enter their waking consciousness, pushing them to change and grow. Resistance is a natural human tendency, and in its more modest form of prudence, it can be a genuine virtue. But resistance can prevent people from recognizing the deepest, most transformative insights of their dreams, precisely because those insights challenge their normal, accustomed ways of looking at the world. So when the interpretation of a dream seems to reach a "natural" stopping point, the question to ask yourself is this: have your reflections touched on an element of resistance, confronting you with ideas, feelings, or memories you are reluctant to think about? If you can simply pause for a moment and sit in silence with that question, you may find that out of the silence there emerges yet another dimension of dream meaning, insight, and self-revelation.

CHAPTER 3

JOURNEYS

Passing Away

Death is not the end. It is rather a new beginning, a mysterious movement from individual bodily life to something beyond.

This is the testimony of countless pre-death dreams that make creative use of the death-as-journey metaphor. Dreams of traveling, passing, moving, changing locations, and crossing from one place to another are remarkably common, and they help the dying person anticipate what lies ahead, envisioning the momentous transformation to come. The imagery of the dream speaks directly to the person in his or her particular life context, and the emotional impact is often tremendous—a fundamental shift from fearful despair to calm acceptance and even welcome expectation.

This is what happened to Bill, the ship's captain we discussed in the Introduction. His dream of sailing at night in uncharted waters stimulated within him a "tingle of excitement" and spirit of adventure that countered his depression over the inevitably fatal conclusion to his illness. The dream took Bill back to a special time in his life when he also faced the vast unknown, while steering cargo ships at night through the South China Sea. In so doing, Bill's dream metaphorically prompted him to make a connection between the spiritual trust he felt *then* and the spiritual uncertainty he is experiencing *now*. "I feel ready to go," he said after the dream, "More so every day." To dream of death as a journey is to reorient oneself toward the future, beyond the end of bodily life, out into new realms of being and becoming.

This powerful dream metaphor can take many different forms, each of which conveys important shades of meaning and distinctive details relevant to the dreamer's life. In this chapter we will consider several examples of pre-death dreams involving the death-as-a-journey theme, looking at both the cross-cultural patterns and the personal life concerns embedded in the dreams. Of course, you may never have a dream exactly like the ones described here, but we suggest that whatever dreams you do have will make much more sense when viewed in light of the experiences of other dreamers.

The Last Dream of Socrates

A good way to make the point about the cultural specificity of death-as-a-journey dreams is to step outside our contemporary world and look at the experience of someone from a very different time and place. To take an especially vivid example from the earliest days of Western history, the ancient Greek philosopher Socrates told of a remarkable dream he experienced just days before his execution by the authorities of Athens. Socrates was in prison for the two crimes of corrupting the city's youth (by challenging conventional values and beliefs) and advocating the worship of new divinities (that is, the daemon or "divine something" he said gave him personal guidance). Basically, Socrates was in trouble for living the life of a true philosopher. His friends and students desperately wanted him to escape into exile, and they had a plan to help him do so, but Socrates would not leave, refusing to repay the injustice of Athens against him with his own injustice against the city's laws. Normally a person convicted of such charges would be executed immediately, but the day before Socrates' trial began Athens had sent a ship on an important religious mission. Until the ship returned, the city had to maintain a state of religious purity and could not perform any executions. So Socrates sat in prison, patiently awaiting the ship's return, and the day of his death.

One morning, about a month after the trial, Socrates woke up in his prison cell and found his good friend Crito sitting there. Socrates asked, "Why didn't you wake me up?" Crito answered that Socrates looked so comfortable sleeping that he couldn't bear to awaken him with the bad news. People in a neighboring city had just seen the sacred ship sailing past, meaning that it would likely arrive in Athens that very day. Here is what Socrates said, as recorded in Plato's dialogue *Crito*:

> SOCRATES: Well, Crito, I hope that it may be for the best. If the gods will it so, so be it. All the same, I don't think it will arrive today.
> CRITO: What makes you think that?
> SOCRATES: I will try to explain. I think I am right in saying that I have to die on the day after the boat arrives?
> CRITO: That's what the authorities say, at any rate.
> SOCRATES: Then I don't think it will arrive on this day that is just beginning, but on the day after. I am going by a dream that I had in the night, only a little while ago. It looks as though you were right not to wake me up.
> CRITO: Why, what was the dream about?
> SOCRATES: I thought I saw a gloriously beautiful woman dressed in white robes, who came up to me and addressed me in these words: "Socrates, to the pleasant land of Phthia on the third day thou shalt come."
> CRITO: Your dream makes no sense, Socrates.
> SOCRATES: To my mind, Crito, it is perfectly clear.[32]

At one level, Socrates' dream appears to be a prophetic revelation, indicating how closely connected Socrates was to the realm of the divine. But there are other elements to the dream that reveal further levels of significance regarding his attitude toward his imminent death. One of these elements is the line, "To the pleasant land of Phthia on the third day thou shalt come." Recalling our earlier discussion about the importance of specific details in dreams, the question to ask here is, why are *these* particular words used to convey the prophecy? The line is not a random one; it happens to be a direct quote from Homer's epic poem *The Iliad,* which we could describe (anachronistically) as the "bible" of the ancient Greeks. At one point in the tale Achilles, the greatest warrior of all, is tempted to give up the fight, and he says that in three days of sailing he could journey back to his home of "fair Phthia," where he left behind a life of pleasure, prosperity, and comfort. But when his best friend Patroklos is suddenly killed by the Trojans, Achilles in his rage changes his mind, returns to the battle, defeats the Trojan champion Hektor, and is soon thereafter killed himself.

For the ancient Greeks, Achilles was the ideal image of masculine virtue, a mighty warrior who sacrificed happiness (the life of Phthia) for the higher ideal of honor in battle. When Socrates' dream used this particular quotation from *The Iliad,* it was comparing him to this major cultural figure, and striving *through* that comparison to anticipate the meaning of his own death. Like Achilles, Socrates was facing death deliberately, with courage and conviction, willing to yield his life for a greater and nobler cause. But unlike Achilles, Socrates was perfectly at ease with his decision. While Achilles agonized over conflict between the goodness of Phthia and the glory of battle, Socrates suffered no such emotional split. For him, dying with dignity and sailing to fair Phthia were one and the same thing. Death could not extinguish the happiness that came from a philosopher's life devoted to truth and justice.

Another crucial element in Socrates' dream is the figure of the woman. She speaks to him in the dream with the same sense of trustworthiness that Socrates had found throughout his life with his "daemon." But while his daemon was merely a voice, Socrates' dream presents him with a voice and a body —and not just any body, but a gloriously beautiful female body, clothed in radiant purity. For an aged man standing at death's door, there could hardly be a lovelier or more reassuring way of inviting one to embark on this mysterious voyage into the realms of existence beyond mortal life. The woman is the divine embodiment of Socrates' final philosophical insight, that his death is a creative act, the greatest affirmation of the principles to which he had devoted his life.

We will say more in the next chapter about the guiding figures who appear in pre-death dreams. For now, we want to highlight in Socrates' story the fundamental theme of the journey, with its specific image of sailing by ship. The dream connects the ship of Achilles with the Athenian ship whose return to the city will mark the day of Socrates' death. Imagining death as a journey by sea is a recurrent theme throughout history, and at one level it reflects the powerful allure of the ocean—the open horizon, the rhythmic breaking of waves, the rich, salty smell in the air—these are qualities that naturally stimulate thoughts of eternity. At another level, the sea journey metaphor reflects the prominent role that sailing has played in human cultural development. From the far-flung roamings of the Polynesians through the South Pacific to the aggressive raids of the Nordic Vikings across the northern Atlantic, from the Arctic travels of the Eskimo to the colonizing circumnavigations of European sailors like Columbus and Drake, humans have always been drawn to explore the farthest reaches of the ocean, and what they have found has often radically transformed their understanding of themselves and the world. The vast, seemingly endless expanse of the sea, combined with the promise of surprising changes and potentials for growth, makes a journey by sea an especially apt metaphor for dying. Socrates' dream draws upon that common theme and creatively combines it with a more culturally specific reference to the ultimate destination of his journey. If you or I had a dream of "fair Phthia," it would probably not mean very much. But for Socrates, the beautiful woman's words make perfect sense, using language familiar to him, speaking directly to his personal effort at making meaning in the final days of his life. Death in the form of a ship is coming across the sea *to him,* and he is resolved to meet his fate with dignity and composure.

Modern Transportation

Returning to the present day, several distinctly modern modes of transportation appear in pre-death dreams—trains, subways, elevators, aircraft, and, by far the most frequent, automobiles. Cars play a major role in dream content at many stages of life. For children, dreams of cars and trucks often reflect their waking-world anxieties about getting caught in speeding traffic. For adolescents, dreams of driving can express the greatly expanded freedom that comes with becoming old enough to have a driver's license. For adults, cars in dreams serve as flexible, multifaceted images of one's individual self, with the color, type, age, and condition of the cars metaphorically mapping onto corresponding aspects of the dreamer's personality. The prevalence of cars in dreams should really come as no surprise, since we live in a society where the cars we drive serve as carefully coded communications about our identity, economic status, and value system. When cars appear in dreams, they merge those cultural meanings with the private concerns of the individual's life. So, for example, a dream of riding in a limousine could express a desire for more public attention, a dream of malfunctioning brakes could reflect a waking-life feeling of being out of control, a dream of being stuck in a crowded minivan could relate to problems with one's family. It remains true that only the dreamer can know for sure which metaphors do and do not apply. Still, our cultural language of the automobile is so strong that certain themes and images recur in almost everyone's dreams. Douglas Hollan, a psychoanalytic anthropologist at UCLA, puts it this way:

> What kind of cultural understandings might the image "self as auto" entail? Perhaps the notion that life and people should run smoothly and without interruption; that when life and people do break down, they should be repairable; that life is a journey involving constant movement and progress, and that one is in trouble if one is stopped too long by the side of the road; that big, strong, fast, powerful cars are better than small, weak, slow, broken-down cars; that it's better to be the driver of a car than a passive passenger; that it's better to own a car than not; that one's car is one's castle and its boundaries are sacred.[33]

When we look at cars in pre-death dreams we find all of the above, and more. The car appears as a highly individualized means of making the journey from mortal life to the unknown destinations beyond. The power of this metaphor is all the stronger given the sad waking-world fact that tens of thousands of people die every year in car crashes. To depart from this life by driving in a car makes sense on multiple levels to people in contemporary society.

Scott was a sophomore in high school when a popular senior at his school named Ryan died in a car accident. Although Scott wasn't a close friend of Ryan, he was deeply affected by the sudden death of someone so young whom he knew personally. A couple of months later, Scott began complaining of headaches, and after a series of increasingly alarming tests, Scott's doctor delivered the shocking diagnosis: he had a brain tumor, an unusually fast-growing one that left him only a couple of weeks to live. Scott and his family were stunned, and when Tish first came to visit him in the hospital, the young man was thin, pale, and emotionally numbed. As she and Scott spoke about leaving his family and friends, he told her that what made him saddest was now he would never get his driver's license. From the way he spoke, Tish gathered that Scott was less interested in driving per se than in all the new freedom, social status, and opportunities to impress girls that would have come with a license. It was also clear to Tish that Scott's sadness about the driver's license was a condensed expression of many other causes of terrible sadness. Indeed, people with terminal illnesses often latch onto one particular concern or worry with special zeal, focusing all their emotional energy on it as a way of expressing a variety of other anxieties.

The last time Tish visited Scott his demeanor was noticeably different. "Can you imagine the dream I had?" he asked. Intrigued, Tish shook her head no, and asked him to tell her. Scott said that

> *the previous night he had dreamed that his dead school-mate Ryan was alive again, sitting in a red convertible, offering Scott a ride. Happily, Scott said yes. He got in the car, and away they drove.*

As he described the dream to Tish, Scott said it was the last thing he ever would have expected—and yet strangely, it was exactly what he would have hoped for. The amazing dream gave him a new view of death, and he told Tish he actually felt excited at where the journey was going to take him.

The emotional impact of such a dream is heightened by its distinctive details, in Scott's case the detail of the red convertible. Compared to other types of cars, convertibles are open to the air, the wind, the elements—they're open to the heavens. Convertibles offer a sense of adventure and liberation; they're associated with youth, vigor, and speed. The fact that the convertible is colored red aligns perfectly with these qualities. Colors in dreams are always worth exploring, as they often express feelings, desires, and moods that defy simple verbal expression. Although there is no fixed universal meaning for any particular color, red is perhaps the most widely experienced dream color because of its connection to blood, the physiological precondition for human life. In American culture red is metaphorically connected with passion, life energy, and fiery spirit. Scott's dream connects these qualities with Ryan, the older and more popular student who invites him for a ride in this exciting vehicle. It will be the ride of death, there's no doubt about that with Ryan behind the wheel. But it will also paradoxically be a ride of life, a ride that promises Scott new discoveries and surprising transformations. Just as Bill's sailing dream envisioned death as a journey across the infinite sea, Scott's dream imagines death as a liberating ride on the open road.

Car dreams can also express terrible fears about the passage from life to death. Eighty-four-year-old Margie was in the final days of her life, staying at the home of her daughter Angela. When her doctors told her there was nothing else they could do and sent her home from the hospital, Margie was consumed by fear, turmoil, and helplessness. Early one morning she woke her daughter with frantic, agonizing cries and the repeated words, "There is no driver in the car! There is no driver in the car!" Angela rushed into the room and found her mother trying to grasp the air as she reached out frantically for help. When Margie finally awoke from the dream, she recounted that

> *she had been in a car, but it had no driver and it was going down a field that sloped steeply toward a large ditch that two men were digging. Some of her grand-*

children and other children whom she knew were run-
ning and playing in the field. She kept calling out to
them, only to realize that when they came near they just
looked past her, showing no signs of recognition.

It took Angela all morning to calm Margie down from
the dream, and we can easily understand why. If a car can be a
metaphor of the self, there could hardly be a more terrible vision of impending death than being in a car without a driver,
careening down a steep hill toward an open grave. Margie's
dream adds the further detail of the children who are playing
innocently among themselves, oblivious to her predicament.
This accurately reflected her waking-life fear of being abandoned by her loved ones, of dying alone. Even though she was
now in the care of her daughter, Margie was terrified of being
left by herself to die. Her dream portrays this anxiety by
means of a dramatic opposition. On this side is Margie herself, old, dying, and alone in a doomed car. On the other side
are the children, playing together in a perfect image of life,
vitality, and youthful companionship. Margie's dream shows
death as a kind of journey, but a journey of a wholly negative character. For Margie, dying appears as a total break with
life, annihilating all relationship, a helpless plunge into a pit of
darkness.

In the next chapter we will look at a dream Margie had the
very next night, a dream in which something unexpected entered her anticipatory imaginings, offering her an alternative
vision to that of death as a driverless car.

Subtle Shifts

The dream metaphor of death-as-a-journey can appear in
many different forms, with various types of transportation
and images of the ultimate destination. What all these dreams
share is a sense of death as a passage or movement from one

place to another. In dreams of ships and cars, the movement is envisioned in large-scale terms, across long distances, at great speeds, in powerful vessels and vehicles. In other dreams the movement is more subtle, without any technological assistance, covering less physical space but nevertheless giving rise to an emotional experience of comparable power and impact.

Suzanne was an elderly woman in a hospital suffering the final stages of a terminal disease. One morning she told her doctor she had just awakened from a dream:

> *She sees a candle lit on the windowsill of the hospital room and finds that the candle suddenly goes out. Fear and anxiety ensue as the darkness envelops her. Suddenly, the candle lights on the other side of the window and she awakens.*

That same day Suzanne died, "completely at peace."[34]

The metaphorical image in her dream is as simple as it is profound. She is about to die—what will happen to her then? Will it be painful? Where will she go? To these basic existential questions Suzanne's dream responds with the vision of a candle extinguished, then relit. The candle goes out in her hospital room, and there is a moment of fear and darkness; but then the candle lights again on the outside. The element of fire is believed in many cultures and religious traditions to symbolize the enduring essence of a human being, and funeral rites around the world involve burnings that release the deceased person's soul from his or her body. Suzanne's dream draws on this same metaphorical imagery, showing her death as a movement of flame from inside to outside. The movement does not cover much distance in terms of physical space, and the actual means of passage are not clear, but *somehow* the flame goes on after dying in the hospital room. In the dark space outside the window Suzanne sees the candle revive itself, and it continues burning for her like a visionary beacon. According to the testimony of her physician, this brief but vivid anticipatory dream helped Suzanne approach the imminence of her death without fear or despair.

Life Reviews

Death-as-a-journey dreams can take even more mystical forms. Episcopalian priest and Jungian analyst John Sanford wrote of a dream his father experienced a week before his death. Sanford's father was dying of kidney failure, and he felt humiliated and depressed by the whole ordeal of painful testing and treatment at the hospital. Then one night he had a dream:

> *In the dream he awakened in his living room. But then the room changed and he was back in his room in the old house in Vermont as a child. Again the room changed: to Connecticut (where he had his first job), to China (where he worked as a missionary), to Pennsylvania (where he often visited), to New Jersey, and then back to the living room. In each scene after China, his wife was present, in each instance being of a different age in accordance with the time represented. Finally he sees himself lying on the couch back in the living room. His wife is descending the stairs and the doctor is in the room. The doctor says, "Oh, he's gone." Then, as the others fade in the dream, he sees the clock on the mantelpiece; the hands have been moving, but now they stop; as they stop, a window opens behind the mantelpiece clock and a bright light shines through. The opening widens into a door and the light becomes a brilliant path. He walks on the path of light and disappears.*[35]

Here is a dream that surveys the whole of the individual's life, a panoramic sweep across time that ultimately leads to the *cessation* of time. Sanford's father reviews the major stages of his life, with his wife a steady companion from the moment he first met her in China all the way to the end of his days, when the doctor pronounces him dead and the clock on the mantelpiece stops. But while the chronological journey of bodily life may have finished, the dream envisions the beginning of a new kind of journey, along a timeless path of brilliant light. Sanford wrote, "My father knew of course that this was a dream of his approaching death, but no longer did he have any anxiety. When he died a week later it was in complete peace; he fell asleep at home and 'forgot' to awaken. We had a special stone marker made for his grave—it has etched into it the 'path of light' down which he went."[36]

Just Wish-Fulfillments?

People throughout history have noticed that dreams tend to revolve around our deepest wishes and desires. Freud based his psychoanalytic theory of the mind on the idea that when a very strong wish is frustrated in waking life, people will dream about it at night. Dreams like those of Socrates, Scott, Suzanne, and Sanford's father would seem to be perfect examples of Freudian wish-fulfillment dreams, in that they offer the promise of some kind of life after death. The wish is the primal desire of any organism not to die, and the dreams fulfill that wish with fanciful images that deny the finality of death. Freud took a dim view of such dreams because he felt they revealed an infantile unwillingness to face the cold, hard facts of reality, and he argued that people could achieve true emotional maturity only by renouncing their wishes, surrendering their happy but illusory dreams, and devoting themselves instead to a rational mastery of the physical world.

Although we agree with some of Freud's insights about dreaming, we disagree with his dismissive claim about wishful dreams. The extremely vivid and memorable dreams we have been discussing did not diminish the individual's abilities to face waking reality. Rather, the dreams enhanced them, as Socrates, Scott, Suzanne, and Sanford's father felt markedly less fearful and more hopeful *after* their dreams than they had before. The emotional power of their dreams strengthened their adaptive resources at just the moment when they needed help the most. If these are wish-fulfillment dreams, they are wish-fulfillments in the service of greater courage, vitality, and wisdom.

This point was illustrated in a remarkable way in Tish's work with a middle-aged woman named Ruth. A hospice counselor asked Tish for help with Ruth, who had only a few weeks to live and who was extremely anxious and increasingly agitated. Her Christian faith, which had been a hugely meaningful part of her life since childhood had, in her words, "just up and disappeared." Nothing made sense anymore. She was worried sick over what to say to her pastor of many years, and she was angry that now, just now, when she really needed it, her religious faith had vanished. The hospice counselor asked Ruth if she would be open to a visit from Tish, and she said yes. So Tish went to Ruth's home the next morning, and she was surprised at Ruth's apparent lack of pain and high level of energy. Ruth said she had a kind of cancer characterized by little ongoing pain but a rapid decline in the end. Her doctor had recently told her she was experiencing the onset of that decline now.

At the beginning of their conversation Tish said she was the person from the hospice patient care team who was particularly interested in spiritual matters, with training as an interfaith minister. She told Ruth she had no particular message to bring, but she was willing to listen if Ruth wanted to talk about what was happening with her religious faith. Ruth laughed a little self-consciously and said, "Well, I don't know. You'll probably think what I'm going to tell you is just awful and want to leave." Tish shook her head a little, smiled, and replied, "Don't worry, I won't leave. What's going on?" There was a long pause, then Ruth heaved a great sigh and began to speak.

Ruth had been brought up in a family of committed Protestants and had learned her faith in an old-fashioned Sunday school from kindly teachers. She had loved God and believed the stories in the Bible. Ruth's family had been poor and hard hit by the Depression. However, they had managed somehow, and had been relatively happy in the process. Her parents placed a high value on education, and through hard work and sacrifice each child in the family eventually had been given the opportunity to go to college. Ruth majored in literature and all through the years continued to read good books and show an interest in new ideas.

She had also continued her religious practices. She attended the local Methodist church on a fairly regular basis. When her children were young she taught Sunday school. Occasionally she took part in church-related projects. She knew the current pastor quite well and was planning to have him conduct her memorial service. But now, all of a sudden, her religious beliefs had evaporated and she was beside herself. How could she die without God? Was there no heaven after all? She wasn't even sure she wanted a Christian funeral, something she knew would upset everyone. "I'm scared to death," she said as she finished, and she buried her face in her hands.

After a pause, Tish asked her if she could remember what was happening at the time she first noticed her faith changing. Ruth said she had been reading some books on Buddhist spirituality and one in particular by a "guru type," as she described him. "All of a sudden it didn't seem possible that God could be captured in any earthly frame of reference. All we can know is a Presence, that's it, a 'Creative Presence.'" At that point Ruth started to cry again, and then she sobbed, "I've lost it all. What am I going to do? Now that I've told you I bet you don't want to talk to me anymore."

Tish took Ruth's hand in her own for a few moments. Then she said, "Ruth, I do want to talk with you. I know this has been very hard for you. Let's just take it slowly together. Maybe things aren't quite as bad as they seem. Because of the nature of faith, a crisis often signals the beginning of new growth." While listening to Ruth it had occurred to Tish that she was probably in just such a time of faith development, and rather than losing her faith completely as she feared, she was more likely to be undergoing a transformation of her relationship with the divine, an expansion of her spiritual perspective on life and death. Ruth's body noticeably relaxed as she and Tish discussed her feelings in these terms. "I guess I just need to let these new ideas about the Presence unfold within," she said, and Tish agreed. They ended their time together for that day and made plans to meet again in three days.

When Tish arrived for their next meeting, Ruth opened the door as she was ringing the bell, and ushered her into the living room. Before Tish was fully seated Ruth said, "Something's happened! I've had a dream, in fact I've had the same dream three times in a row!"

"Tell me about it," Tish said.

Ruth explained:

It was the same dream every night just as I went to sleep. There were several huge, deep blue boulders with eerie blue lights pulsating from them. They made a very loud wailing sound. All my attention was riveted right there. It was frightening, no, awesome, no, really frightening. Then I was awake again. The image of the boulders was gone, but all I had to do was close my eyes and it was back. And yet I didn't have a hard time going back to sleep. This happened three nights in a row.

Tish asked Ruth if she could say anything else about the noise. "It was very loud and crashing," Ruth replied, "like whole mountains were moving. It didn't make me afraid I would be hurt. But it filled every possible space where noise could be and just engulfed me."

"Can you describe the color and how it moved?"

"The blue was very deep, almost purple, and had a metallic quality. Very deep and very blue, the most blue of blue. And it pulsated, sort of danced like the northern lights. It was alive and compelling. Those boulders were awesome. And that was it. It sounds so simple as I tell you, but it was truly incredible to experience."

"What do you make of it? Does anything come to mind as you remember the dream?"

"It was like drums beating so loud that you think they are your heartbeat. It was the Presence, whatever that means. Not the boulders themselves or the noise itself. The Presence was all around. I was spellbound."

"The Presence?"

"Yes, it filled my heart and soul. I felt saturated, and then the whole thing faded. And there's something else. After the second night I called my daughter, Julie, on the phone and told her about the boulders. She called me back the next morning to say that she had had a dream about boulders, too. In her dream the boulders were stone gray and there wasn't any accompanying noise. Isn't that amazing? Imagine us sharing this dream! I feel like we're closer together."

Tish continued to visit Ruth every few days, as the cancer took its course. Despite the mounting pain, Ruth felt increasingly comfortable with her transformed understanding of God as spiritual Presence, and she reveled in the fact of God's great freedom in the vastness of space. "I don't need to know anything more than that," she said. "God is God, that's all that matters." Ruth even invited her pastor over and told him of her new spiritual insights. To her great relief, he was supportive of her, and together they planned her funeral.

On the day before Ruth died Tish visited, knowing it was

time to say goodbye. Ruth was very weak and could hardly speak. She paused every moment or two to let Tish lightly brush her lips and teeth with cool water on a swab.

"Tish," she whispered, a faint but unmistakable smile on her face, "I had the boulder dream again last night."

They had flattened into stepping stones and had moved to make sort of a path and were singing sweetly like the gentle wind. In the distance was a soft, inviting, clear golden light. It was the Presence calling me.

She paused, and looked into Tish's eyes. "It's calling me now, and I want to go. The curtains no longer keep out the light. Nor the walls. It's here with us now. *The light is right behind you....*"

Wherever Ruth's final dreams and visions ultimately came from, it's clear they had a strongly positive effect on her dying experience. Her "wishes" were not really fulfilled, at least not in any orthodox way. What she received was something different, a stunning revelation of transcendent energy beckoning her onward. Rather than defending her against the harsh reality of dying, Ruth's dreams led her *forward* into death, welcoming it as a natural necessity and a profound spiritual transformation.

CHAPTER 4

GUIDES

Light

In Ruth's dreams the journey itself becomes a force of guidance. The glowing blue boulders are transformed into a path that leads her onward, inviting her to move toward the golden light of "the Presence." Then, at the very end of her life, Ruth realizes the light is all around her, right there in her room, calling to her. This same image of light-as-divine-guide also emerged in the dream of John Sanford's father, when a bright light shines through from a window behind the stopped mantelpiece clock, revealing a "brilliant path" that draws him forward, away from this world. Suzanne's dream likewise draws on the powerful metaphorical connection between light and spiritual guidance beyond death, though in a relatively humble manner—as a little candle extinguished then relit, rather than an eternally burning cosmic brilliance.

The recurrence of the theme of light in pre-death dreams corresponds with the same phenomenon widely observed in near-death experiences, such as the perception of a vivid light at the end of a tunnel or pathway, to which one would go if one actually did die. Various explanations of this have been offered in relation to near-death experiences. Some researchers have pointed to naturalistic causes, such as oxygen deprivation, neural dysfunction in the limbic region of the brain, and side effects from psychoactive medications, while others have argued that the visions of light reflect a universal core to near-death experiences, revealing the archetypal reality of death for all humans.

Our experience with pre-death dreams suggests that light is a frequently occurring element, but not a universal one. We definitely believe there is more going on in these dreams than simply the hallucinatory malfunctioning of the brain. At the same time, we do not claim they reveal any objective insight about what happens beyond death. We prefer to view these dreams as especially powerful metaphorical expressions, as creative visions of what it will be like to pass from living to dying. Most of the world's religious traditions, and certainly the Abrahamic traditions of Judaism, Christianity, and Islam, closely associate the essence of God with light. Anyone who is born and raised in these traditions is culturally predisposed to envision the divine in luminescent terms. Putting the same point slightly differently, this religious metaphor of light-as-divine-guide is likely to wield a profound influence on the dreaming imaginations of people in these cultures, providing a familiar and ready-made language by which to seek greater understanding of what death will bring.

Surprisingly, this is a place where religion and science find some measure of agreement. Many living creatures display heliotropism, a reflexive tendency to orient toward the sun. Certain animal species have been observed performing "solar rituals" in which they sing, call, and/or move in response to the rising and setting of the sun.[37] The existence of virtually every biological organism on the planet depends on consuming substances that have, in one way or another, absorbed the energy of the sun. Humans, with our exquisitely evolved visual system, have an enormous capacity for processing information through subtle patterns and variations in light. If, as some neuroscientists claim, visual awareness is the central feature in the rise of human consciousness, then we can truly say that light is the origin of a fundamental sense of self.

All of this scientific evidence indicates that the brilliant light of the sun has played an enormous role in human evolution, and thus it is eminently natural to make metaphorical connections between light and the ultimate source of terrestrial life. The many religious traditions that revere the divine light are, in scientific terms, tapping into a primal condition for our biological existence. In religious terms, the phenomenon of heliotropism in both plant and animal species can be seen as a protospiritual yearning for communion with God. Either way one looks at it, the light-as-divine-guide metaphor is deeply rooted in who and what we are.

Companions on the Journey

Light is not the only guiding force in pre-death dreams, however, and in this chapter we will describe other guides who appear in pre-death dreams, sometimes in conjunction with light imagery and sometimes independent of it. We have already discussed a few dreams with particularly striking guide figures, including Socrates' dream of the gloriously beautiful woman and Scott's dream of the older high school student Ryan. Light plays a role in both of these dreams—the woman is wearing a white dress, suggesting radiance and purity, and the redness of Ryan's car is a vivid presence that reflects a sense of energy and vitality. However, the power of these dream guides involves more than visual illumination—it emerges from the specific details of their words, gestures, and personal interactions with the dreamer. Knowing more about guide figures who appear in pre-death dreams is a crucial element in caregiving for the dying because encounters with these figures open a direct channel to the dying person's emotional condition and spiritual preparedness. Even though the dream encounters may be labeled "imaginary," the feelings they stimulate are real enough, and anyone involved in caregiving practice can benefit from taking them seriously.

Family Visitations

Aunt Jo lay dying in the hospital. She had lived a hundred and three "wonderful years," as she described them, and had told her family many times that she was "ready to go." Her nephew Richard was sitting at her bedside watching over her as she slept. Slowly her eyes opened, and with growing recognition she looked at him first with astonishment, and then with a gathering sadness.

"But you can't be here, you can't," she whispered.

Richard, now feeling her concern himself, leaned closer and said, "But I am here, right next to you. What's the matter?"

"Grandpa Will, Charlie, Aunt Kate, and Aunt Francis are all here, come to get me. But it's not your time yet. Why are you here with us?"

Startled, Richard said, "Look, it's me. I'm the only one here." He took her hand in his and added kindly, "You're fine. Everything's just fine."

After Aunt Jo's funeral a week later, Richard told other family members about what she had said, and they wondered what it could mean. Was Aunt Jo going crazy, becoming confused in her final days, losing her ability to distinguish fantasy from reality? Or was she really perceiving the spirits of various deceased relatives who had come to lead her onward?

These are questions we cannot answer in any definitive way. We may, however, develop a better understanding of what happens *within* these dreams and visions, that is, their images, characters, bodily sensations, and felt qualities. We may also gain a better appreciation for their positive emotional impact on the dreamer, dissolving fear and engendering hope in the midst of dying. Aunt Jo's waking dream offers a simple illustration of this. She doesn't see just anyone, as if it were a chaotic, disorganized hallucination. Rather, she sees those family members who were close to her earlier in life and who are now dead. As we discussed in Chapter 1, visitation dreams frequently involve the vivid, highly realistic reappearance of close loved ones who have died, and these are the same type of characters that appear most often in the dreams of the dying as guides for the journey ahead. From the perspective of the dreamer, these characters have held trustworthy positions in the dying person's life and now have direct experience of what's involved in making the passage from life to death. The emotionally positive impact of pre-death visitation dreams is evident in Aunt Jo's reaction upon awakening, when she is surprised to see her nephew Richard. What strikes her as strange and troubling is *not* the presence of several deceased family members, but the one living, physical body in her room. The "spirits" are comforting and welcoming, and Aunt Jo accepts their invitation. Richard, though, is not supposed to go yet, and Aunt Jo is momentarily worried about his welfare. For herself, she feels nothing but a calm readiness.

The blurring of boundaries between dreaming and waking is not necessarily a sign of mental deterioration. In fact, it is a regular characteristic of intense, highly memorable types of dreams such as visitation dreams. If caregivers do not listen carefully to what the dying person is saying, they very well might miss a vital expression of pre-death insight and revelation. This is especially true in hospitals and other healthcare institutions, where busy attendants are often unfamiliar with the life background of the dying person. What initially sounds like the disordered ramblings of dementia may turn out to be courageous efforts to articulate powerful spiritual experiences that, whatever their ontological status as "real" or "illusory" occurrences, are profoundly meaningful to the dying person, and may even provide some measure of consolation to the person's family and friends.

Margie's Second Dream

For many people, the journey of dying simply cannot proceed without the presence of a reliable, caring guide. Recall Margie's "driverless car" dream from the last chapter. Not only is it a bleak vision of death as a journey to nowhere, it portrays her as frighteningly alone, without any guidance or companionship, with no one behind the steering wheel of her car. This was a terribly upsetting dream for Margie, as it gave full voice to all the emotional turmoil and anxiety she felt in anticipation of her impending death.

The next morning, however, when her daughter Angela went in to check on her, Margie was awake, refreshed, and quiet. She told Angela she'd had another dream:

> I was alone, walking home from a dance hall, feeling isolated, dejected, and sad because no one had asked me to dance. As I came nearer my house, my father appeared, opened his arms wide, and gave a wonderful, loving hug. We walked home arm-in-arm.

Margie said the dream gave her "such a comfort," and to Angela's great surprise, her mother was no longer scared of her impending demise. "I think I'm ready to die," Margie told her. A few days later she did pass away, without fear and at peace.

The appearance of Margie's deceased father transformed what had started as another dream of rejection and isolation into a deeply felt experience of spiritual reassurance. In the dream Margie can't find anyone to dance with her—she can't, metaphorically speaking, find anyone who will be her spiritual companion while she dies. She is aware of other people dancing, just as she was aware in the first dream of the children playing in the fields. Margie senses the vitality around her, she still feels a tenuous connection to youthful energy, but she fears her death means being cut off from that energy forever. Then her father appears, and everything changes. His welcoming embrace—the kind of direct physical contact that many dreamers say is incredibly realistic—washes away all of Margie's fears. *She is going where he already is,* to the comforting familiarity of the family home. Just like a child, she had been feeling weak and vulnerable, but now her father is with her, providing the longed-for warmth of parental care and protection.

For a woman raised, as Margie was, in the religious ethos of the Protestant Midwest, the image of her father walking her home would be felt and understood through the lens of her Christian faith, where "father" is God and "home" a heavenly place of safety, acceptance, and love. Death may constitute the ultimate rupture with youthful vitality—moving decisively *away* from the playing children and the people dancing— but thanks to the guidance of her father, Margie finds herself emerging into a kind of new spiritual childhood that beckons her onward. The feelings and insights from this dream clearly carried over into Margie's waking life in a very powerful way. She felt loved and accepted by her father/Father and comforted by the vision of being taken home. Her attitude toward death changed from fear and agitation to peace and connectedness.

Pre-Death Dreams as Religious Experience

It is worth pausing for a moment and reflecting on the key qualities shared by the dreams of Margie and the others we have been discussing. These dreams combine vivid, highly memorable imagery, strong emotional sensations, and a sense of being connected to extraordinary figures and realities. By almost any measure of the term, the dreams can be understood as religious experiences, with the same transformational power associated with the mystical traditions of many of the world's religions. William James, in *The Varieties of Religious Experience,* pointed to this feeling of transpersonal relationship as a cardinal feature of mystical experience:

> [The individual] becomes conscious that this higher part [of the self] is coterminous and continuous with a MORE of the same quality, which is operative in the universe outside him, and which he can keep in working touch with, and in a fashion get on board of and save himself when all his lower being has gone to pieces in the wreck.[38]

This is exactly the experiential quality of the dreams we have been describing. James showed that religious experiences cannot be dismissed as aberrant, abnormal, or pathological. He rejected this "medical materialist" view and argued instead that such experiences reflect, in psychological terms, the extraordinary operation of the subconscious regions of the person's mind. Ordinary waking consciousness is only one of many possible states of awareness, James said, and people who have religious experiences are giving us testimony from *other* modes of consciousness that are different from but not automatically inferior to our usual waking state.

What James said in 1901 has been amply confirmed in the century of psychological research since then on the unconscious dimensions of the human brain-mind system. We now know that a vast amount of psychological functioning goes on outside of ordinary consciousness, and we know that "religious" phenomena such as dreams, meditation, prayer, and visualization involve a dramatic reorganization of the brain, producing different modes of knowing and different experiences of self-awareness. The evidence is clear that people who have such experiences are for the most part healthy, functional individuals who, for reasons that remain poorly understood, are able to shift significantly the balance of their brain-mind operations, bringing into consciousness what is ordinarily unconscious.

Having said that, James goes on to note that the psychological concept of the subconscious only explains what is happening on the "hither" side of religious experience, close to our current state of ego awareness. What may be happening on the "farther" side, in the distant realm of possible divine, transpersonal realities, is a matter of metaphysical debate rather than scientific proof. When scientific materialists say there are no such transpersonal realities, they are offering what James calls an "over-belief," a statement of metaphysical conviction that has the same status as a theologian's argument for the existence of God. Both are visions of ultimacy, efforts to conceptualize the fundamental nature of existence and thus to make greater sense of what it means to be human.

The best way to test these visions, James said, is to evaluate their fruits, looking at their tangible, practical effects in people's lives. Judged in these terms, pre-death dreams deserve a place in the highest ranks of religious experience, because their emotional impact on people is so frequently positive and (paradoxically) life-affirming. This transformational power, combined with the striking images of the journey and spiritually charged figures of guidance, makes pre-death dreams a legitimate type of religious experience that closely relates to mystical phenomena found in many of the world's great religious traditions.

To recognize the mystical dimensions of pre-death dreams is not necessarily to glorify them or to suggest that those who have such dreams are "spiritually better" than those who don't. There is no one right or proper way for people to die—everyone's journey is unique and true to his or her specific life context. What we want to highlight is the fact that pre-death dreams are natural, healthy expressions of the dying person's imagination and are worthy of greater attention from caregivers. It really shouldn't be a surprise that most people, when they reach the final days of their lives, start thinking and wondering about questions of ultimate meaning, value, and purpose. The dreams and visions that come in response to those questions should be honored and celebrated, not ignored or rejected. It is perhaps a sign of American society's "denial of death" that pre-death dreams are, despite their great frequency, so rarely mentioned or acknowledged by healthcare professionals responsible for the daily care of the dying. Obviously one of our goals in this book is to change that attitude.

Following the Children

Margie's dream of coming home from the dance and being embraced by her father highlights another prevalent theme in pre-death dreams, that of children and childhood. Margie's initial feelings about death echo the almost universal fears and anxieties of children who worry about the threat of abandonment, isolation, and vulnerability. Her second dream presents her in the position of a child being reassured by her parent. This image in turn echoes the teaching of many religious traditions (particularly Christianity and Buddhism) that new spiritual growth depends on the renewal and cultivation of a childlike sense of openness, trust, and simplicity. What Freud pejoratively labeled "regression" can actually be a movement *forward* in terms of faith development. In this way, the child becomes a powerful guide for the dying person.

Jim had lived a life of power and privilege. He had been a successful businessman and community leader. Now, at the age of fifty-two, during what he thought would be the prime of his life, a degenerative disease had suddenly struck him down and left him with only a few more days to live. He was angry at fate for dealing him this terrible blow, and he found the loss of control in his life unbearable. He was anxious and agitated nearly all the time. His wife, Helen, was beside herself trying to keep him comfortable and dealing with his angry outbursts. Through a reference from hospice she called Tish and asked her to visit. Helen said Jim had had a dream and she wondered if Tish might be able to help him make sense of it.

When she arrived, Jim was very pale and hardly had the strength to speak. Slowly, in a soft, halting voice, he told Tish his dream.

He was a little boy in the schoolyard of the town where he had grown up in the Pacific Northwest. He and some children were playing a circle game, which had moves almost like square dancing. As they moved toward and away from each other in the dance, Jim could see images of the lines of connections like colorful ribbons making patterns. That was it.

Tish waited, rightly sensing that Jim had his own ideas about what the dream might mean.

He looked at her, and said with a tiny smile, "There really is a plan after all, isn't there? I didn't believe it. But it was there all the time."

"Tell me about the pattern," Tish asked.

Jim paused for quite a time. Then he said, "Somehow we all belong to one another. None of the rest of it, the physical things and objects that surround us, none of it really matters."

He waved his hand around the room, as if brushing away all the insignificance from his world. He paused again, and said one more word.

"*Imagine . . .*"

He lay his head back on the pillow of his bed and closed his eyes, a smile still on his face.

It seemed clear to Tish that Jim had interpreted his dream as opening new dimensions of meaning in his life. The cancer had destroyed his confidence in the meaningfulness of the world. Without the proud badges of work and leadership status, his self-esteem had shattered and he was consumed by anger. Life was unfair, unjust, and certainly not benevolent. But now, because of this dream, a newfound understanding of life and death had emerged. Thrown by the illness into a state of childlike helplessness and vulnerability, Jim (like Margie) discovers in the dream of returning to childhood a dramatically new and emotionally transformational insight into the magical web of relatedness that embraces us all. His boyhood self must lead his fifty-two-year-old self to remember what his big-shot businessman persona was no longer capable of imagining. Jim doesn't go into elaborate detail about what the pattern looks like—what matters to him is the realization that the meaningfulness of life is *real* and will survive his individual death, and he no longer has to worry about losing his ultimate connection to the pattern.

Many psychologists, philosophers, and religious studies scholars have pointed to meaning making as a primary motivating force in human life. Jim's experience reflects the power of pre-death dreams to generate startling new developments in our sense of living in a meaningful world, and this leads to another important correlation between these dreams and the world's religious traditions. Huston Smith has written eloquently about this dimension of religion and spirituality, and he affirms Immanuel Kant's philosophical premise that all human thought, belief, and experience is inescapably shaped by the limited range of our senses and the inherent biases of our minds. As a result, we never know reality "as it is," but only an indirect version of reality that we have creatively imposed upon it. The great question, Smith says, is whether there are any meanings in the world that transcend these human limitations. This is precisely what the world's religious traditions have always been seeking:

Beginning with the conviction that Kant was on the right track in regarding the human mind as a pattern-making instrument, we posit a comparable propensity in the human spirit to work its life experiences into meaningful patterns exemplifying the categories of trouble leading to hope, to endeavor, to trust, and ultimately to mystery. Meanings are not given to experience but received from it. Therefore, the meaning man senses his life to possess is neither forced upon him by facts nor subjectively contrived.[39]

Thinking of Jim's experience in these terms, his dream and his interpretation of it can be seen as an example of how the spirit, like the mind, is a "pattern-making instrument" that takes in perceptions of the world and creates a meaningful reality out of it. Although Jim couldn't see any trustworthy meanings from his adult point of view, he could still find his way back to the wellspring of his creative imagination thanks to the guidance of his childhood self. As a direct result of the dream, Jim realized that life's deeper significance lies in a pattern of exuberant, playful relatedness. His wife, Helen, and the rest of his family were surprised and relieved to find that Jim now felt a considerable lessening of fear and a new sense of comfort and peace as death approached.

Following the Elders

The guiding figures in pre-death dreams most often come from the other end of the life span, from our beloved elders. Teachers, healers, spiritual leaders, and grandparents figure prominently in dreams while they are alive and, even more powerfully, after they have died. As noted earlier, grandparents frequently appear in visitation dreams, and such dreams can now be seen as early anticipations of what, for the dying person, is a looming reality.

Hiroshi was only twenty-eight years old when a diagnosis of lung cancer left him just a couple of months to live. When Tish first called on him, he was very frightened and confused, and desperate for help. His sister, who lived nearby, was his primary caregiver. Their parents had moved to America from Japan in the 1960s, and Hiroshi and his sister were the first generation of their extended family not born in Japan. As Tish spoke with them she gathered they both were Christians of a rather conservative nature, well-educated, and neat but not fussy. Hiroshi said his main fear was that because he had chosen to become Christian as part of his Western enculturation—which he said he was doing intentionally and enthusiastically—he was going to die and enter the next world to find his Japanese ancestors angry with him. Hiroshi was suddenly terrified at the realization of his own rebellion from his family's religious beliefs, and he worried that now he might have ruined his chance for a happy afterlife. He had given up his family's traditional ancestor worship, and now he was going to pay the price.

The reassurances from his sister, Tish, and everyone else who visited Hiroshi were well intentioned, but none of them could persuade the young man that he wasn't going to suffer a horrible punishment in the afterlife for his disrespectful behavior in this life. Then, about a week before he died, Hiroshi had this dream, which he described as unusually vivid and detailed—"It was so real that it must have happened!":

> The doorbell rings, and I answer it. There stand my aged grandparents, very short, neatly dressed, bowing and smiling. They slip off their shoes in the traditional way, enter the room, and hold forth two very large bouquets of pinkish orchids. I bow deeply and smile in return at their happy faces. I accept the bouquets, and that was the end of the dream.

This generational reconciliation produced a dramatic emotional change not only in Hiroshi but also in his sister and the rest of their family. Before Hiroshi died everyone knew about his dream and expressed awe and amazement at his spiritual communication with the venerated grandparents, who had both died many years before. The dream became a shared symbolic creation giving voice to fears, regrets, wishes, and hopes felt by all of them. It reassured them that no matter what different paths their lives took, they were all still loved and appreciated by the family as a whole. Tish was asked to participate in Hiroshi's memorial service, and when she arrived, there was a table set up at the front of the mortuary chapel with large vases of pink orchids surrounding an eight-by-ten-inch photo of Hiroshi.

Hiroshi's dream thus served as a healing force not only for him personally but also for all the other relatives who were struggling with their own experiences of tension and conflict between their traditional culture and the relentlessly destabilizing forces of modernization. Indeed, this kind of conflict is endemic in the contemporary world—all of us are increasingly subject to the violent tugging and pulling of multiple cultures, identities, and value systems. "Globalization" is only the latest term for a process that has been accelerating since the early twentieth century, and we are all living through an era in which spectacular innovations in transportation and communication technologies have brought *more* people into contact, *faster* and more *violently,* than ever before in history. All over the world, traditional ways of making meaning have been challenged by an unavoidable confrontation with *other* ways of making meaning, other views of human nature, other spiritual orientations, other yearnings for power and vitality.

These conflicts regularly play out in people's dreams. To an extent researchers are only just beginning to understand, our dreaming selves are fully *cultural* beings, immersed in the languages, metaphors, social patterns, political hierarchies, legal rules, religious rituals, and moral teachings that govern our waking lives. To be sure, in dreams we frequently violate cultural boundaries by committing immoral acts and breaking sexual taboos, and this is another reason why dreams have always had been viewed with suspicion and mistrust. But even in these cases, the dreaming self is engaged with the cultural world in an oppositional sense, acting in defiance of what is considered normal and proper.

Indeed, transgressing traditional moral boundaries can be seen as the precondition for creativity and the resolution of seemingly impossible problems and conflicts. The creative power of dreaming derives in large part from the freedom we have while asleep to explore, in a safe and harmless environment, those areas of our cultural world where we feel most troubled and confused. The images and feelings that emerge have the beneficial effect of reorienting the dreamer's sense of selfhood, clarifying important truths and integrating previously alienated elements of identity.

This is what happened in Hiroshi's dream. Despite the fact that he and his sister had, in waking life, turned away from the religion of their ancestral culture, Hiroshi's dream envisions a surprising reconnection with that seemingly abandoned spiritual community. What was feared lost forever is suddenly found—and turns out to be a present, living reality, thanks to the welcoming guidance of his grandparents.

The dream could be seen as a rejection of Hiroshi's Western Christian identity, but that would only be true of a narrow kind of Christian faith that rejected all other religions and denied any other way of relating to the divine. Hiroshi and his sister did in fact belong to a church whose minister preached in rather exclusive terms about the superiority of Christianity to every other religion. This only added to Hiroshi's anxiety because he understood the minister's message to be that he had to cut off all connection with the traditional values and beliefs of his family. His dream speaks directly to this anxiety by offering him a vision of a broader integration of *all* the elements of his identity—his past, his present, and his future. The gift of the pink orchids is a gesture of friendliness that bridges the fearful divide in Hiroshi's identity and unites the Christian and Japanese Buddhist influences in his life. His family wisely incorporated the flowers into his memorial service, honoring this final gift of creative vision from Hiroshi's dreaming imagination.

Family and Faith

Conflicts between different religious beliefs within a family and between friends frequently come to the surface when a person is in the last stage of a terminal illness. Hiroshi's dream visitation from his grandparents helped him overcome one such conflict. Another young person who was dying, a close relative of Tish's and Kelly's named Tracy, experienced a similar difficulty when a close friend of the family made a religious comment that, while meant to be helpful, in fact caused great emotional pain. Like Hiroshi, Tracy received a surprising dream visitation in which family and friends who had already passed away were beckoning her to come join them.

Tracy was only twenty-five when she was diagnosed with leukemia. During a terrible, up-and-down year of tests, treatments, and hospital stays, Tish was fortunate to have several good visits with Tracy. One night while the two of them were sitting together at the old family beach house, Tracy began opening some of the cards and letters she had received from people expressing their sadness over her illness. One of the cards really angered her, and she read it aloud to Tish. The letter came from a family friend who told Tracy she was getting sicker because she wasn't praying fervently enough. Just pray harder, this person said, and God will cure you. Tracy became so furious she started to cry.

A couple of weeks later, as the end approached, Tracy was asleep in her hospital room, with her mother sleeping next to her on a visitor's couch. Tracy suddenly stood up and started walking around the room. Her mother awoke to the sound of tubes and IVs dangling along with her, and she jumped up from the couch to check on her daughter. Tracy woke all the way up at that point, and exclaimed, "Oh, I thought I was in the beach house bathroom." She then told her mother about the dream she had just had.

At the beach house people were at the card table in the family room playing some sort of game—they all had masks on—and some voices outside the room, or above it, kept calling her name and saying, "Come with us, come with us, Tracy." They were laughing and singing and having a good time. "Don't worry about them," she was told about her other relatives at the game table, "What they don't know won't hurt them." Tracy was in the family room of the beach house as this was happening, and the party seemed to be going on in the direction of the living room, where the fireplace is. But she could not go through closed doors between the two rooms, so she had to go down the hall near the bathroom to get into the other room where the party was going on.

Her mother was astonished, and asked if Tracy was scared by the unseen party from which the strange mixture of voices was coming. Tracy said, "No, not at all—they seem happy and joyful." In reaction to the phrase, "What they don't know won't hurt them," Tracy said she felt it meant that if we humans knew how wonderful the next world was going to be, we wouldn't want to stay in our bodily lives on earth.

The dream helped Tracy set aside the unthinking comment that implied she was making her own situation worse by not praying sincerely enough. The person who wrote the upsetting

card made it sound like dying was a sign of God's disfavor—
if you pray hard enough you won't die, so if you *do* die, if you
just happen to be struck at an early age by an incurable disease, it must be evidence that God does not want to heal you.
A very different message comes through in Tracy's dream,
which portrays her dying as a passage beyond ordinary physical barriers to a new realm of joy, energy, and kinship. Death
is no longer a curse of spiritual doom, but a warm invitation
to a reunion with the people she loves. Like everyone else who
grew up spending sunny summers at the beach house, Tracy
had vivid memories of her older relatives and family friends,
now deceased, playing card games at that very game table in
the family room. To be welcomed by those beloved elders into
the happy playfulness of their otherworldly fellowship was,
for Tracy, a powerful reaffirmation of her own faith that God
loved her absolutely, just as much in dying as in living.

CHAPTER 5

OBSTACLES

Auntie's Visit from Her Mother

Lynn and her sister Madeline were providing home care for their Aunt Sheila ("Auntie"), who was dying and in her last days. Auntie was grouchy and difficult to be around, growing ever more so as the time of death approached. She complained about everything, constantly made sharp, critical comments to her nieces, and rejected any efforts to provide her with physical comfort and emotional support. Things became so bad that Lynn and Madeline did not even want to get near Auntie because she was so angry all the time. One morning very close to the end, Lynn went into Auntie's room and found her strangely changed. When Lynn asked how she was doing, Auntie cheerfully replied that her mother (Lynn and Madeline's long-deceased grandmother) had just been in her room for a visit. They had a wonderful time talking together, Auntie said, and all of a sudden she was happier than she had felt in a long time.

Worried that Auntie was becoming delusional and detached from reality, Lynn said surely she had been dreaming. After all, Lynn's grandmother had been dead for many years. Instantly the fury returned to Auntie's voice. "NO!" she declared, "It was not a dream, it really happened." Increasingly alarmed, Lynn tried to persuade her it must have been a dream, but Auntie insisted just as forcefully that her mother *really had visited her.* Auntie started hitting the bed with her hand to show Lynn where her mother had sat. "She is coming for me," Auntie announced, and that was the end of the conversation.

Lynn told Madeline about what Auntie had said, and Madeline felt just as skeptical and concerned as her sister. "Auntie's losing it," Madeline said, and Lynn couldn't help but agree. They both took Auntie's apparent inability to separate fantasy from reality as a frightening sign of impending mental deterioration. Though her body might stay alive a little while longer, they feared that Auntie's mind had begun the irreversible slide into senility, and she would no longer be able to function meaningfully in their world.

But to their great surprise, Auntie did not "lose it." In fact, over the final week of her life Auntie's behavior changed very much for the better. She was no longer so relentlessly grumpy and irritable. On the contrary, she became happier, more peaceful, even eager. Her abilities to think, perceive, and communicate remained in fine shape, and she became cooperative with Lynn and Madeline in their care of her. When she finally died she left Lynn and Madeline with amazing memories of a "new Auntie," a kind and courageous soul whose powerful vision of her deceased mother "coming for her" gave her nieces a new insight into dying. As Lynn and Madeline told other family members after the funeral, Auntie's experience had changed them forever. They knew Auntie was fine, wherever she was, and now they themselves were no longer afraid of death.

If dying can be understood metaphorically as a journey from this life to a destination beyond, the various difficulties surrounding death can be seen as obstacles along that path. In this chapter we look at pre-death dreams as a source of insight into the obstacles often faced by people who are dying. Auntie's experience illustrates several such obstacles. One is her intense anger, an emotional bitterness so strong it led her to push away her nieces and everyone else. Her attitude was this:

If life is rejecting me, then I'm going to reject life. This kind of reaction to the realization of one's own dying is perfectly natural, for a while at least. If it hardens into a constant state of hostility, however, it can block any possible growth or development in one's final stage of life. Caregivers, being on the receiving end of this hostility, are often at a loss as to how best to respond. Though they desperately wanted to help Auntie, nothing Lynn and Madeline could do or say had any effect on her stubbornly negative attitude. It took her intense visionary encounter with her deceased mother to break through that angry shell, reconnecting Auntie with a new source of trustworthy guidance, a reassuring presence that would lead her through the inevitability of death.

Another obstacle that's illustrated by Auntie's experience is the difficulty of distinguishing between dreaming and waking reality. For Auntie, her visit with her mother was absolutely real. For Lynn and Madeline, however, it must have been a dream. Who is right? In many cultures and religious traditions around the world, these two claims would not be seen as mutually incompatible. Waking reality is not believed to be the *only* reality; a dream or vision can be real, too, just in a *different* way from waking experience. This pluralistic way of thinking is hard to accept for many people in modern society, where any mode of consciousness that deviates from the rational waking state is viewed as pathological and worthless. Such an attitude poses a serious impediment to a full appreciation of the value of pre-death dreams. In the case of Auntie, the unmistakable change in her behavior persuaded Lynn and Madeline that *whatever* she had experienced, whether a dream, vision, hallucination, or something else entirely, it was deeply meaningful to her and as emotionally "real" as anything could be.

This is a point worth emphasizing. The intensity and vividness of certain dreams can be so great as to leave the individual genuinely unsure of what exactly happened—people say the experiences are so striking and unusual they're not even sure the word "dream" applies anymore. As we have noted, many of the world's religious traditions teach that such dreams are a valuable means of connection with the divine, while a modern psychological view would regard them as unusually strong products of unconscious brain activation. Whatever your belief system, the common element here is the *emotional power* of these dreams. Whether or not Auntie's mother really visited her, and whatever we want to call the mode of consciousness in which Auntie perceived her, the experience was emotionally real, and had real behavioral consequences. By any reasonable standard of evidence, Auntie's attitude was transformed from a negative to a positive state. The experience had a beneficial impact on her, and this is exactly what James says of religious experience—*what are its fruits?* In what practical ways did it change the individual for the better? We want to highlight the emotional transformation produced by pre-death dreams and visions, a transformation that reveals an ever-present growth potential at the end of human life, even in one's final days and hours. Caregivers should never forget that such potential always remains within the dying person, no matter what condition they are in, no matter how cruelly they speak, no matter how belligerently they behave.

A third kind of obstacle appears in Auntie's experience, or rather in her effort to communicate her experience to Lynn. The friends and family members of a dying person are almost always suffering terrible emotional distress themselves as they try to prepare for the imminent loss of their loved one. Indeed, sometimes the dying person reaches a point where he or she feels calm, content, and ready to go, while the family members may *not* be ready for the person to go and may instead be desperately holding on! This was definitely the case with Auntie. After her visionary experience she was eagerly looking forward to joining her mother, but Lynn was terrified at the prospect of Auntie "losing her mind" and leaving them forever. Fortunately, Auntie had just enough time left to relieve her nieces of that fear, by showing them that *she* wasn't scared. Rather than mentally deteriorating and losing contact with reality, Auntie became more fully engaged with reality, more lovingly bonded with her nieces, and more mentally stable than she had been before. Eventually Lynn and Madeline came to share Auntie's brave acceptance of death, and thus they were in the end able to let her go.

Family Traditions, Family Barriers

As the story of Auntie suggests, the obstacles dying people confront may include the beliefs and expectations of their families and friends, including their religious beliefs. As we discussed in Chapter 1, the world's religious traditions have developed many different approaches to death and dying, and each tradition provides its members with specific ideas about what happens at the end of life. For many people, these religious teachings provide valuable guidance, and they are a welcome addition to caregiving efforts. For other people, though, the teachings do not correspond very well with their personal experiences, with the specific details of their own unique passage from this life. In these cases the religious teachings do not provide guidance for the dying person's journey, but rather impede it. Family members may be offering what they think are words of spiritual comfort when they are in fact emotionally hurtful. Tracy's story in the last chapter is a good example of this.

Pre-death dreams can play a crucial role in the process of dissolving the conflict, overcoming the obstacle, and pointing the way forward in the journey ahead. One of the wonderful things about dreaming is the way it zeros in on the special personal concerns of the dreamer, speaking directly to his or her life situation right here, right now. When a dying person is feeling overwhelmed by family and/or religious expectations about certain events or activities that *must* occur before death (whether the dying person wants it or not), a dream may come that offers an opening to another way of approaching death, an alternative route to that given (or imposed) by the family's religious tradition.

Rosemary was the seventy-four-year-old matriarch of a large and devoutly religious Italian family. She had been diagnosed with terminal cancer, and after her doctors told her they could do nothing more to stop the disease, she left the hospital and returned home to the care of her husband, Paolo. When Tish came for a visit, one of the first things Paolo told her was that Rosemary would not die until the Blessed Virgin Mary appeared at the foot of her bed. He said that it had to happen that way because it always did in his family, and this time would be no exception. Tish took note of that familial religious expectation, and when she sat down with Rosemary, she found the dying woman very quiet. Paolo answered most of Tish's questions for her, repeating the family's beliefs about heaven and the afterlife. He clearly had a very definite idea about what the journey from this life to the next would be like. What Tish could not yet tell was whether *his* vision of the journey was the same as Rosemary's, and whether his expectations were unintentionally posing an obstacle in her dying process.

One day Tish had a chance to sit with Rosemary alone, and Rosemary told her a dream. She had been at a huge Christian gathering in Candlestick Park (the nearby professional sports stadium), and the Pope was in the middle of the field on a high dias saying Mass. The stands of the stadium were full of people singing and praying with the Pope. Somehow Rosemary realized that under the altar there was buried treasure. While the Mass continued above her, Rosemary went below the altar to the place where, buried in the ground, a treasure of gold lay waiting. She awoke with the awareness that this hidden gold was hers for the finding.

Tish did not offer a formal interpretation of the dream, nor did Rosemary request one. The two of them simply sat together and marveled at the dream's imagery and emotions, as Rosemary wondered at the strange feeling that somehow *she* was the gold, that she was the treasure and the treasure was her... and all of this happening "under" the Pope, below the awareness of the religious authorities, and out of sight of all the other faithful Christians. Rosemary had discovered her own unique source of spiritual value and worth, and she knew where that source was leading her.

After Rosemary passed away, Tish spoke to Paolo and he proudly told her that yes, Rosemary saw a statue of the Blessed Virgin Mary at the foot of her bed, and they had all been able to say goodbye to her before she died.

Tish never knew if Rosemary had actually seen the Virgin, or if she had just told her forlorn husband what he wanted to hear, or if Paolo had made the whole thing up to satisfy the obligations of the family tradition. What she did know, however, was that Rosemary's dream generated a tangible sense of comfort and enthusiasm, relieving her of any sense of pressure or inadequacy and affirming the special dignity and worthiness of her own individual path of dying.

Dreams, Visions, and Dementia

Many people suffer serious mental deterioration in the course of dying. A number of different diseases have the effect of disordering and/or destroying the neural functioning of the brain. With this in mind, we want to be clear we are not suggesting that every word a dying person says should be taken as a divine revelation. Indeed, the friends and family members of a dying person may fervently *wish* to hear some glimmer of meaning or communication from their psychologically disabled loved one, and thus be tempted to read great spiritual significance into gestures and utterances that are nothing more than the tragic symptoms of dementia.

Nevertheless, an honest appraisal of a dying person's mental condition should not rule out the possibility of sudden moments of visionary clarity and insight. Dementia may be a devastating obstacle in the journey of dying, but even if a person's disease has seemingly incapacitated his or her mental functioning, the capacity for powerful spiritual experience may still be there. A pastor friend of Tish's told her of the death of James, a sixteen-year-old who was diagnosed with a fast-growing cancer that in just a few weeks left him in a coma. Just before he died, and with his family gathered around his bed crying and praying for him, James suddenly opened his eyes and, with a look of what everyone took to be rapture, he lifted his arms upward for an extended moment. Then he lay back down, and a few minutes later he was gone.

This is not an uncommon experience. Similar moments of startling clarity also occur with some people who are suffering from Alzheimer's disease. Just before death, when their psychological functioning seems almost entirely ruined, they may spontaneously experience a flashing moment of recognition, a brief but meaningful burst of awareness. It's as if the person's mind had managed to pull itself back together for just one final instant of integrated presence in the world, the soul gathering back to the body as the last step of this life and the first step of the journey ahead.

Caregivers are well advised to listen for indications of such experiences and acknowledge them if and when they occur. Again, not everything a dying person says is spiritually meaningful, but not everything they say is random nonsense either. The art of caregiving in both religious and secular contexts is being able to discern the difference, and respond accordingly.

Of course, it is likely that most pre-death spiritual experiences occur without anyone other than the dying person knowing about them. This is especially true of dreams, which cannot be directly observed by anyone outside the individual. We can only know about other people's dreams if they *tell* us about them, and for that reason we are very limited in what we can know about the possible dream experiences of people who are suffering severe impairments in their language abilities. Neuroscientists have recently discovered that REM dreaming involves a different pattern of brain activation than is found in waking awareness, and this means that a dying person may be dreaming just fine, but without the ability to express or communicate the dreams in waking language. Indeed, we believe the vast majority of pre-death dreams occur in this way—real and meaningful to the dreamer, unknown to everyone else. What else can we say about people who die in their sleep? Their final dreams have led them to, and across, the bridge separating life from death.

Painful Secrets

The rapid approach of the end of life inevitably brings old, painful memories back to mind. Secrets that have been long denied, harsh truths that have been fervently resisted, lost opportunities that still hurt—all of this and more come roaring back, threatening to overwhelm the dying person with a psychological hurricane of images, feelings, and conflicts.

Dreaming is one of the ways we try to recenter ourselves in the midst of such swirling, stormy emotions. According to Ernest Hartmann (one of the great elder statesmen of dream research), an important function of dreaming is *making connections* between present concerns, past experiences, and future anticipations.[40] Because dreaming occurs without the constraints of focused waking consciousness, the mind is free to make wider, more far-ranging connections during sleep than is possible while awake. Dreams help restore some degree of stability and integrity to the self, even if that requires the painful step of openly admitting our worst fears and most terrible regrets. The old self, the self that lived in denial of all those dark secrets, inevitably crumbles in such dreams. But the genius of our dreaming imaginations is that a new self is always being created out of the ruins of the old. What the dying person experiences in waking life as an agonizing onslaught of painful memory becomes, in dreaming, the raw material for new growth, broader connections, and a deeper sense of self-integrity.

The remainder of this chapter will describe two cases of people approaching death whose dreams helped them overcome severe conflicts in both their external relations (their families, religions, cultural communities) and their inner lives (their memories, emotions, desires). Surrounded in waking life by obstacles, barriers, and impediments, these two people found in their dreams a source of guidance leading them through and beyond the process of dying.

The first case is that of a young gay man named Christopher, a patient of Jungian analyst Robert Bosnak who wanted help escaping his homosexuality—his initial complaint to Bosnak was, "I don't want this gay life anymore."[41] Christopher was raised in a fundamentalist Christian community, and he attended a Bible college in the South with plans to become a minister. He was popular and successful in school, and for a time was even engaged to be married to a close friend named Ava. But after a thought-provoking trip to the Soviet Union, Christopher decided he didn't want his life to be predicated on a lie. He broke up with Ava and told the college what he himself had known since early adolescence—he was gay. The school immediately expelled him, and he moved to Florida and threw himself into the "fast gay life," working as a salesman in the fashion industry and becoming "totally promiscuous." This is the life Christopher wanted out of, and he turned to Bosnak for guidance.

The only dream Christopher could remember at their first meeting was a tiny fragment:

Visit Aunt Lib. I have to cross to the other side.

Christopher drew a blank in response to Bosnak's question about Aunt Lib, who was a distant friend of his grandmother and never really a part of his life. Perhaps, Christopher said, her appearance in the dream had something to do with liberation, as in "women's lib" or "gay lib." The dream might thus be acknowledging that he could be liberated from being gay, and cross over from the gay side to the straight side. Bosnak wasn't so sure, but admitted he had no alternative explanation of his own: "What is this desire to get away from being gay? The mysterious urgency behind it forces the dream into a single optic. All he can see is his desire to leave the gay life. Why? And crossing over to the other side—what's that all about? I have no idea."

Christopher's second dream involved a frightening journey on a boat:

Dream of driving around something like a lake on a white speed boat. I'm not driving and feel as though I could be thrown off and should possibly take control and drive. We come to a place where we have to go through and a weasel of a small wiry man charges us to go through. It is some sort of a passage, but not a lock. I paid it but remember feeling he charged too much (embezzled me) and feared I would not have enough for later.

Bosnak realized this dream repeated the theme of going to the other side, of crossing from one place to another. Christopher saw this as further confirmation of his desire to leave the gay world, while Bosnak couldn't help focusing on the little weasel man who's charging an exorbitant fee for the passage —a discomforting image of the "analyst as rip-off artist." Bosnak, one of the most insightful dreamworkers in practice today, acknowledged the obstacle posed by his own reactions: "With some effort I tell myself that I am getting trapped in a trait of my own, making me unable to look at the dream." Bosnak allowed those personal anxieties their due place in his awareness, but he then went back to focus anew on Christopher's efforts to make meaning out of his troubled situation.

Over the next several sessions Christopher reported other dreams in which there was a marked emphasis on vertical, up-and-down movement. Combined with the first two dreams of horizontal crossings, the impression emerged for Bosnak that "this is a dreamscape of undertows in all directions." There's lots of movement, but no clear direction or destination. Additional dreams included becoming lost and disoriented at a school, losing his place in a play, and riding a bike down a slippery path.

If you have read our book to this point and learned about the common patterns of pre-death dreams, you will probably not be surprised at what happened next. Christopher began having health problems, went to a medical doctor, and was diagnosed with AIDS. When he reported this to Bosnak, the news violently shattered the resistance both of them had been feeling against this looming reality. Christopher's urgency to leave the gay world could suddenly, in retrospect, be understood as a panicked unconscious reaction against the illness that had already taken root in his body. Bosnak said, "His initial dream—'I have to cross to the other side'—now shines in an altogether different light." All the movement in his dreams, the crossings and vehicles, the obstacles and disorientations, now appeared as metaphorical expressions of what he unconsciously *knew* was happening. Here, as in many cases, the dreams were far ahead of the dying person's conscious awareness in terms of preparing for what's to come.

Over the final months of his life Christopher continued seeing Bosnak and sharing his dreams. Images of the journey continued, with many variations on the theme of obstacles blocking his way. In one, he's in a car and the steering wheel is on the right side rather than the left, leaving him unsure whether he'll be able to drive "on the opposite side." In another dream his car runs out of gas, and in still another he's being driven by people who fall asleep at the wheel while driving a hundred miles an hour. A more positive image comes in a dream where he's riding an elephant with his former fiancée, Ava. The elephant then changes into "a wonderfully beautiful antique open carriage," metaphorically reflecting Christopher's reconciliation with a very important person from his past. Although he decided not to join with Ava on the traditional path of heterosexual marriage, Christopher can now look back at his time with her and appreciate the goodness of their friendship.

Christopher's dreams had few other guide figures in them, most likely because Bosnak himself was serving that role in his waking life. The last dream Christopher tells him envisions the final trip Christopher must ultimately take by himself, and what he may find along the way:

I'm in my convertible driving down to the river. There's a party down by the river. Lots of people are milling about. The atmosphere is busy and fun. I walk into the crowd. But it is as if no one is noticing me. I am completely on my own, walking through a crowd of people who don't seem to see me. I feel isolated. Then I see in the mud a tiny little gold coin. I pick it up. It is extremely precious and has triangles on it. Triangles within triangles.

Christopher has indeed left the fast, partying life he once led, but his "liberation" is much more profound than he initially expected. He is no longer a part of the gay crowd, or indeed of any community of this world. He's becoming invisible, immaterial, a disembodied presence, totally isolated from other people. But then he discovers the coin, a small but precious bit of treasure. This of course echoes the dream of Rosemary earlier in this chapter, when she finds the gold buried under the Pope. As a metaphor, finding treasure in the earth is a wonderful expression of surprising discovery and good fortune—a classic fairy-tale affirmation of the worthiness of whatever journey a person is making. For Christopher, the tiny gold coin is an emblem of ageless value. The coin appears incredibly small to him (analogous to the brief life of a young man cut down by AIDS), but he perceives an enduring worthiness in it, a beauty that defies being lost and buried in the muddy ground.

After Christopher died, Bosnak decided to write out a chronicle of their work together. The night before he began to write Bosnak dreamed this:

> I am in a camp of Outward Bound. We have to learn to go through dangerous terrain. I'm with my teenage son. I have to go down a very narrow rocky shute. I am terrified. The most terrifying thing I can think of is going down a very narrow shoot and getting stuck, like those children in Dickens's time who were sent up the chimney to clean it, only to find themselves getting stuck, never to move again. I stand in front of it and dare not go through it. Next to us, over on our left in the green grass among the rocks, there is another shute. This one is smaller and smoother. It is for children. My son looks sad. He says, "I live with others; dying I do alone." Then he goes down the shute.[42]

This is the kind of dream that people who care for the dying might well find themselves experiencing. The obstacles in the journey of dying block the way not only of the dying person but his or her caregivers, too. Their own fears about death are inevitably triggered by their efforts on behalf of the dying person, and these fears may threaten to paralyze the caregivers emotionally, to the point where they feel stuck, immobilized, frozen with anxiety. Perhaps the greatest challenge for caregivers is being able to accept the fact that the dying person must eventually go on, *alone*—leaving the caregivers behind with the mournful task of trying to make sense of a world that suddenly has a huge, agonizing hole in it. Dreaming contributes to this emotional work of mourning by giving the fears a vivid imagistic form, as in the narrow rocky shute in Bosnak's dream. Such images give us a clear, honest perception of our deepest fears, and this has the beneficial effect of activating our unconscious powers of creativity and healing. Bosnak's dream ends with words of irrefutable worldly wisdom, from the unlikely source of his teenage son—"I live with others; dying I do alone." At a certain point, the living can no longer continue, and must say goodbye. For this caregiver, who gave everything he could to a dying young man, the dreams they shared and influenced in each other became a part of his own journey of living and dying.

Dying for Her Faith

The last story to share in this chapter concerns one of the most remarkable dream documents in all of Western history, the diary of a young Roman woman named Vibia Perpetua. In 203 C.E. Perpetua, living in Carthage, the second city of the Roman empire, was imprisoned and sentenced to death for refusing to renounce her Christian faith. She was twenty-two years old, newly married, and mother to an infant son. Her father repeatedly begged her to do what the Roman authorities were asking. If only she would agree to make a few meaningless public gestures and statements, her life would be spared and her child would not lose his mother. Perpetua, though deeply moved by her father's passionate pleas, would not deny her faith. Like many other Roman people who had recently converted to Christianity, Perpetua believed her relationship with God superseded any worldly power or authority, making it impossible for her to bow in reverence to the emperor. So she waited in prison, still nursing her infant son, for the day when she and several other Christians would be cast into the Carthage arena and killed by wild beasts.

In these final days of her life Perpetua kept a diary in which she described a series of four remarkable dreams. The first came after her brother (also a Christian) visited her in prison and told her to ask God for a vision to reveal her fate.

> *I saw a ladder of tremendous height made of bronze, reaching all the way to the heavens, but it was so narrow that only one person could climb up at a time. To the sides of the ladder were attached all sorts of iron weapons; there were swords, spears, hooks, daggers, and spikes; so that if anyone tried to climb up carelessly or without paying attention, he would be mangled and his flesh would adhere to the weapons.*
>
> *At the foot of the ladder lay a dragon of enormous size, and it would attack those who tried to climb up and try to terrify them from doing so. And Saturus [a Christian friend also sentenced to death] was the first to go up, he who was later to give himself up of his own accord. He had been the builder of our strength, although he was not present when we were arrested. And he arrived at the top of the staircase and he looked back and said to me: "Perpetua, I am waiting for you. But take care; do not let the dragon bite you." "He will not harm me," I said, "in the name of Christ Jesus." Slowly, as though he were afraid of me, the dragon stuck his*

head out from underneath the ladder. Then, using it as my first step, I trod on his head and went up.

Then I saw an immense garden, and in it a grey-haired man sat in shepherd's garb; tall he was, and milking sheep. And standing around him were many thousands of people clad in white garments. He raised his head, looked at me, and said: "I am glad you have come, my child." He called me over to him and gave me, as it were, a mouthful of the milk he was drawing; and I took it into my cupped hands and consumed it. And all those who stood around said: "Amen!" At the sound of this word I came to, with the taste of something sweet still in my mouth.[43]

Perpetua was not suffering from a terminal disease. Like Socrates, she was going to be killed by an oppressive government, not an incurable illness. She was not seeking to die, but neither was she scared of death. Her vision of God had become the core of her being, and no bodily threat or mortal danger could stop her from freely worshipping the divine as she felt she must. Her dream portrays a stunning allegory of the obstacles blocking her journey of dying, with her faith a powerful means of overcoming those obstacles and reaching her ultimate destination. Her Christian friend Saturus ably serves as her guide, leading her up a fearsome ladder that many commentators have likened to the ladder spanning earth and heaven in Jacob's famous dream vision at Bethel (Genesis 28). All the horrible weapons on the ladder foretell a journey that will be violent and bloody, while the huge, menacing dragon embodies the primal threat of being destroyed by inhuman evil. Perpetua's faith is strong enough to surmount that fear, however, and the dream brings her to a place "above" all that, where she is free to join her fellow believers and worship God.

In a detail of special significance, the dream leaves her with the tangible sensation of something good and nourishing, a sensation that carries into her waking awareness and leaves her feeling even more self-assured and hopeful than before. Very few dreams involve the senses of taste or smell. Visual and auditory sensations are by far more frequent, and in only a tiny fraction of dreams do people smell and/or taste anything. The strong, positive taste sensation at the end of Perpetua's dream enhances the overall memorability of her experience and gives her an extraordinary awareness of the *reality* of her faith, at a time when that faith was being put to its ultimate test.

When Perpetua told her dream to her brother the next day, they both agreed it was a clear omen of her coming death and ultimate salvation. Nothing more is said about the specific detail of the type of food she consumes. Some translators render the word as "milk," but other translators use "cheese" or "curds," suggesting that Perpetua is speaking of a more solid kind of food. It is interesting that later in her diary Perpetua writes with happiness and relief that her child had started eating solid food, thus removing the last physical bond that held her to this world. This developmental achievement of Perpetua's child parallels her own impending transition from life to death. The Christian community of Carthage ate milk and cheese along with the bread and wine of holy communion, so Perpetua would have readily understood her dream's ritual of nourishment and its metaphorical implication that just as a baby's physical growth is measured by the transition from mother's milk to solid food, so Perpetua's death will be a kind of spiritual growth involving a transition from this life to the next.

Her next two dreams involve her brother Dinocrates, who died some time earlier at the age of seven from a horrible cancer of the face. Perpetua had been praying with the other Christians in prison awaiting execution, and suddenly the name of Dinocrates sprang from Perpetua's lips. Thinking this might be a burst of prophetic insight, she began praying for her brother, and soon thereafter had a dream about him:

> *I saw Dinocrates coming out of a dark hole, where there were many others with him, very hot and thirsty, pale and dirty. On his face was the wound he had when he died.... There was a great abyss between us: neither could approach the other. Where Dinocrates stood there was a pool of water; and its rim was higher than the child's height, so that Dinocrates had to stretch himself up to drink. I was sorry that, though the pool had water in it, Dinocrates could not drink because of the height of the rim. Then I woke up, realizing that my brother was suffering.*

As Joyce Salisbury has pointed out in her excellent book on Perpetua, this second dream illustrates a shift in the young woman's caregiving perspective from the earthly to the heavenly, from the thirsty needs of her child to the thirsty needs of her dead brother. Perpetua shared the Christian belief in the power of intercessory prayer, particularly from those about to be martyred for the faith, and she devoted herself to trying to help her brother in his troubled passage from this life to the next. The dream illustrates the theme of obstacles in pre-death dreams—here, the abyss that separates Dinocrates and Perpetua, and the unreachable height of the pool of water that prevents the hot and thirsty boy from drinking. Perpetua is confident that her prayers can reach across the abyss and aid her brother in satisfying his thirst, and her efforts are rewarded by a third remarkable dream:

> *I saw the same spot that I had seen before, but there was Dinocrates all clean, well dressed, and refreshed. I saw a scar where the wound had been; and the pool that I had*

seen before now had its rim lowered to the level of the child's waist. And Dinocrates kept drinking water from it, and there above the rim was a golden bowl full of water. And Dinocrates drew close and began to drink from it, and yet the bowl remained full. And when he had drunk enough of the water, he began to play as children do. Then I awoke, and I realized that he had been delivered from his suffering.

This third visionary experience continues Perpetua's process of reconciling herself to death and preparing for what's to come. She is reassured by her brother's startlingly positive appearance and his youthful energy. As we have seen in several dreams, this one envisions dying in metaphorical terms as a kind of childhood, as the beginning of a new stage of life, a new kind of existence. Dinocrates has entered a transcendent realm very different from earthly reality, where a magical golden bowl ensures that no one will ever go thirsty again.[44] Perpetua's attention continues to shift from the social relations of this world (the Romans, her father, her child) to the social relations of the next (God, fellow martyrs, her brother). This is also something we have seen before, and Perpetua's case highlights the anguished reaction of the dying person's loved ones as they desperately resist the impending separation. The day before her execution, Perpetua's father visited the prison and tried one last time to turn his daughter back from death. His pleas were in vain. Perpetua wrote in her diary that she took pity on the old man's unhappiness, but she could do nothing other than what she was doing. That night she had her final dream:

Pomponius the deacon came to the prison gates and began to knock violently. I went out and opened the gate for him. He was dressed in an unbelted white tunic, wearing elaborate sandals. And he said to me: "Perpetua, come; we are waiting for you." Then he took my hand and we began to walk through rough and broken country. At last we came to the amphitheater out of breath, and he led me into the center of the arena. Then he told me: "Do not be afraid. I am here, struggling with you." Then he left.

I looked at the enormous crowd who watched in astonishment. I was surprised that no beasts were let loose on me; for I knew that I was condemned to die by the beasts. Then out came an Egyptian against me, of vicious appearance, together with his seconds, to fight with me. There also came up to me some handsome young men to be my seconds and assistants.

My clothes were stripped off, and suddenly I was a man. My seconds began to rub me down with oil (as they are wont to do before a contest). Then I saw the Egyptian on the other side rolling the dust. Next there came forth a man of marvelous stature, such that he rose above the top of the amphitheater. He was clad in a beltless purple tunic with two stripes (one on either side) running down the middle of his chest. He wore sandals that were wondrously made of gold and silver, and he carried a wand like an athletic trainer and a green branch on which there were golden apples. And he asked for silence and said: "If this Egyptian defeats her he will slay her with the sword. But if she defeats him, she will receive this branch." Then he withdrew.

We drew close to one another and began to let our fists fly. My opponent tried to get hold of my feet, but I kept striking him in the face with the heels of my feet. Then I was raised up into the air and I began to pummel him without as if I were touching the ground. Then when I noticed there was a lull, I put my two hands to-

*gether linking the fingers of one hand with those of an-
other and I thus got hold of his head. He fell flat on his
face and I stepped on his head.*

*The crowd began to shout and my assistants started
to sing psalms. Then I walked up to the trainer and took
the branch. He kissed me and said to me: "Peace be with
you, my daughter!" I began to walk in triumph towards
the Gate of Life. Then I awoke.*

Perpetua's fourth and final dream vision prepares her for
the ordeal of dying that will come to her the next day. The
dream portrays that ordeal as a movement from the prison to
the amphitheater and then to the "Gate of Life." She is guided
in this journey by a trusted leader of her faith community,
Pomponius, who offers her reassurance and spiritual companionship. Even though she must enter the amphitheater alone,
Pomponius will still be sharing in her fight to overcome the
obstacles she will find there. Those obstacles take the shape
of a formidable Egyptian fighter who embodies the earthly
power of pagan civilization and who threatens her with the
ultimate physical peril—violent death. But Perpetua is up to
the challenge. In a transformation that has long puzzled inter-
preters, Perpetua suddenly turns into a man and starts doing
battle with the Egyptian. This bizarre image surely reflects the
sharp gender inequalities between men and women in Roman
society, and Perpetua's change from a woman to a man underscores the radical recentering of her sense of self and identity
as she moves toward death. She is no longer bound by society's limitations on her beliefs or expressions. She can "fight
like a man" against a society that's trying to crush her will and
her spirit. The power of her faith is also strong enough to lib-
erate her from the bounds of gravity, as she rises in the air
to pummel the Egyptian and knock him down to the ground.
Just like in the first dream, when she steps on the head of the
dragon at the foot of the ladder before ascending to heaven,

Perpetua steps on the head of the Egyptian as a sign of her victory over death and as the first step in her renewed movement toward the Gate of Life.

Perpetua died the next day. Her dream diary became a cherished text among the surviving Christians of Carthage, and over the centuries it has continued to attract attention and admiration for its poignant account of courage in the face of death. From our perspective, Perpetua's diary provides a beautiful and moving historical illustration of the images, feelings, and themes so often found in pre-death dreams and visions. Whether or not you share her particular religious worldview, you can hopefully recognize in her story truths that apply beyond her place and time, truths that are helpful in your own journey of dying.

CHAPTER 6

CARE FOR THE DYING

A Broader Perspective

Dreams never come in isolation. They are always part of a life context, woven into the broader tapestry of an individual's overall life experience. The dreams that come before death are, in this regard, no different from any other type of dreaming. They are always part of the dying person's current life context and his or her preparations for death. In this chapter we will widen our focus to look at that whole context of living and dying, and we will discuss the most important general principles involved in caring for people at the end of their lives. Paying close attention to dreams is an important part of this process, but there are many other elements as well. Indeed, the full power and value of pre-death dreaming is best realized when the dying person is being cared for in a safe, comprehensive, and loving environment. The practices and methods we suggest are offered as means of creating that positive caregiving environment, something that will, in and of itself, enhance the dying person's capacity to benefit from any pre-death dreams or visions that might come.

We are specifically addressing this chapter to the dying person—that's the "you" in the following pages. Our paramount goal is to embolden you to take charge of the final days of your life and, to the fullest extent possible, create a meaningful and satisfying conclusion to your stay on this earth.

What Is a "Good Death"?

The basic idea here is to have the weeks and days beforehand to lay the foundation for a "good death." Just what makes up a good death? Several qualities are involved: Peacefulness, control of pain, reflection on important memories (both happy and sad), a sense that loose ends are tied up, intimacy with loved ones, business affairs well arranged, memorial service planned, and perhaps reconciliation with people you have been at odds with. A key element of a good death is a basic sense of *dignity,* by which other people continue to treat you with respect, preserve your privacy, and allow you to make your own decisions about the course of your care. For example, you should be kept informed about when death is coming and what can be expected. You should have control over pain relief measures. You should be allowed to choose where death occurs, whether at home, in a hospital, or somewhere else. You should be given access to emotional and/or spiritual support if you so desire. You should have the final say on who is present with you at the end. And, you should be assisted in making advance directives regarding your financial affairs and other personal business.

We encourage you to add further qualities to your own definition of what will constitute *your* concept of a good death. Everyone is different, and everyone follows his or her own unique path. There is no single, perfectly designed, one-size-fits-all formula for producing a good death. Rather, we are offering in this chapter a variety of practices that can be adapted to your personal circumstances. Choose those ideas that fit, the ones that spark some special enthusiasm in you, and let the others go.

Putting together a team of caregivers is probably the most important task needing to be accomplished in planning for a good death, either for yourself or a loved one. Depending on your situation, your team may include many different helpers, or just a few. Among those people whose professional services you might use are physicians, hospice nurses, social workers, psychiatrists, religious counselors, lawyers, home healthcare providers, and housekeeping services. Along with caregiving professionals, you might include certain friends and family members on your care team, people who can make special contributions to your comfort. Whatever combination of people you choose, the goal is to provide you with the resources you need to face death with peace and dignity.

You are the center of your care team. You are in charge, and we hope you will take a keen interest in your medical and personal care. The terminal status of your medical situation means that oftentimes there will be changes in your condition. Because of this, one of the most important qualities to develop is flexibility. That means making plans that include a willingness to change and adapt. We encourage you to choose one person who can be your primary ally and trusted companion, someone with whom you can talk openly about your needs, concerns, and feelings. This person can help you communicate with hospital staff, family members, and friends, keeping track of things on those days you don't feel up to it.

The old saying goes, "You die as you lived." If you have lived a quiet, relatively simple life, your death will probably be quiet and simple. If your life was a "wild ride," so to speak, your death and the time leading up to it might well reflect that. If you're someone who is very organized and likes strict order in your affairs and in your household, you will probably approach death in the same way. If you figure, "Things just sort of work out," then they probably will with your death as they have in other areas of your life. Most of us fall somewhere between these approaches, and whatever personality style has characterized your life, it will probably characterize your last days and weeks before dying as well.

Whatever your personality and circumstances, you are likely to be confronted by serious and often painful challenges. You are also likely to find surprising openings for new growth. The central notion of this chapter is that you always have the power to act in ways that respond effectively to the negative challenges and take advantage of the positive opportunities. We're not suggesting you try to wish away the many painful aspects of dying. A good death is still *death,* and ultimately there's nothing you can do to change that. But what you can do is move *beyond* a despairing fixation on death as the final extinction of your bodily existence, and try instead to cultivate a view of your dying as the culminating expression of an authentic, courageous human life well lived.

Exploring a Lifetime

Physical care should be a major component of your caregiving, but there is much more beyond that. The realization you are going to die opens up the possibility for looking back on your life as a whole, reflecting on past experiences, relationships, and insights. We encourage you to take this wonderful opportunity (which those who die a sudden, unexpected death do not have) to explore your own life, not only for your own benefit but also for the benefit of others. Very few of us die without any family or friends whatsoever. Most people die in the company of people they have been close to in some fashion. There are several ways in which you can share with these loved ones the story of your life, providing them with a lasting, deeply meaningful memory. Even if you don't think you have much to offer ("Oh, nothing important happened in my life, why would anyone care?"), you will be surprised at how much family members and friends appreciate the life-story gifts you are leaving for them.

Here are some possibilities for creating such gifts of self-reflection:

A family health history. Try writing out a chronology of your physical growth and health conditions, along with what you know of your siblings, parents, and grandparents. Besides giving you a new perspective on the role of health and illness in your life, this can also literally be a gift of life for members of some future generation of your family whose doctors can use this history to help with a diagnosis.

A box of drawings. You don't have to be a professional artist to express your memories and feelings through drawings, sketches, and illustrations. Sometimes a visual image, even if drawn by a shaky, unpracticed hand, can communicate powerful memories. Try drawing a picture of a park, beach, or garden you enjoyed as a child; a floor plan of the house you grew up in; a map of your old neighborhood; portraits of your best friends and closest family members; a vision from your dreams.

A photo/scrap album. Most people have an old box somewhere filled with scattered photos, newspaper clippings, programs, letters, announcements, etc. This can be a good time to look through those pictures and papers and reminisce about especially meaningful moments in your life, events that were crucial in shaping who you became, and homes where you and your family dwelled. You may want to create an album that preserves this material for future generations, offering them a window into times and places they can only know through your eyes.

Family stories. You may not know it, but your memory is a treasure-house of stories about love, conflict, success, disappointment, travel, and discovery. You have probably heard many wise, beautiful stories over the years—a tale about how your grandparents fell in love, perhaps, or how your parents recovered after a terrible house fire, or how a friend acted heroically in a difficult and dangerous situation. So many stories like this, so many simple but inspiring family narratives, are lost when a person dies. You have the chance to record those stories, either in writing or on audio or video tape, for others to enjoy after you're gone.

Eyewitness reporting. Your life has covered a stretch of time in which momentous historical events have occurred —you have seen things that future generations will be intensely curious to learn about. What was happening in the days right after the terrorist attacks of September 11, 2001? What was it like during the "Cold War" with the Soviet Union? How did people feel when the Apollo astronauts landed on the moon in 1969? Pretend to be a newspaper reporter and write or tell someone what you saw and what people's reactions were at that time. Your narration of such an historical event acts like a time machine for other people, carrying them back to historical moments when the world changed in important ways.

Holiday celebrations. As you think back over the course of your life, you will probably notice that you have been following a cycle of seasonal holidays, both religious (for example, Easter, Christmas, Rosh Hashanah, Yom Kippur, Ramadan) and secular (for example, New Years, Fourth of July, Thanksgiving, birthdays, anniversaries). These are often times of special social gatherings and heightened emotions, both happy and anxious. You might ask yourself which holidays have been your favorite, and why. Which celebrations were the very best? You might also consider asking your family and friends to help you celebrate a favorite holiday *right now,* even if it's not the proper time according to the calendar. Have Christmas in July, or Thanksgiving in April—bring out the ornaments and photos, share a special meal, and enjoy the experience of a living holiday tradition one more time. You can be sure that this final celebration for you will become an ongoing part of that holiday's mood and feeling for all the people who survive you.

A chronicle of pets. Think of all the animals that have been part of your family and your life. The cats, dogs, horses, and other nonhuman creatures we share our lives with are often as emotionally important to us as our human family and friends. See how many pets you can remember, what experiences you had with them, what joys and sorrows you shared, and how you felt when they died. You might try putting together a little booklet with pictures of your pets, their names, and a story or two about them. For any children who know you and will be affected by your death, this can be an especially cherished gift.

Create a family tree. For many people, dying brings a renewed awareness of their family connections and where they stand in the unfolding of the generations. You may find it a very meaningful project to create a family tree in which you locate yourself in relation to the rest of your family. Even if you've never been all that close to these relatives (or if you're angrily estranged from them), you may still gain a new perspective on your dying experience by looking at your life in terms of the rich interpersonal web of births, marriages, and deaths by which your family has grown over the years and will continue to grow after you are gone. There are so many possibilities for this project: drawing on paper, embroidering on a tapestry or quilt, created on the computer using special software and the internet. Other family members will likely be eager to help.

Dealing with Your Stuff

You will never see a U-Haul trailer hitched to the back of a hearse. After a life full of getting and spending, none of our material things will go with us when we die. (Though some cultures, most notably the ancient Egyptians, see it differently, as they provide their dead with the equivalent of a moving van's worth of goods and treasure to take on their journey to the land of the dead.) The question of what to do with all your "stuff" is, for many people, a distressingly complex problem that generates rippling waves of confusion, anxiety, and conflict among family and friends. Your ability to prepare for a good death will be greatly enhanced by a modest amount of attention to this question. Ideally you will have your primary caregiver to consult with, but the responsibility for making the final decisions is always yours.

All the things you own, taken as a whole, constitute your estate. Hopefully someone has spoken to you already about the need to plan for the "disposal" of your estate. This terrible legal term is often enough all by itself to send people into despair—"After a lifetime of gathering and collecting all these precious possessions, now they're just going to be *'disposed'* of?" That acute feeling of material loss can be compounded by the realization that so many difficult details need to be considered. Even if you have a relatively simple estate, the prospect of getting it all organized can be daunting.

Here again, your primary caregiver or some other trusted member of your care team can help. An attorney can assist you in writing or updating your will. An accountant working with your lawyer can make sure whatever business and tax issues you have are in order. To the extent possible given your medical situation, try to allow yourself time to make these arrangements so you are satisfied with the outcome. Having accomplished these tasks will contribute greatly to the peacefulness of your last days.

Instead of thinking of all this as a matter of "disposal," try instead looking at it as a celebration of giving and sharing. It can be hard for us in the highly consumerist world of modern society to imagine, but there's a joy and even a profound strength in giving your possessions to others. A striking cross-cultural example of this is the wonderful tradition of the potlatch among the Native Americans of the Pacific Northwest. Members of these communities would try to outdo each other in having grand parties at which the host would give away everything he owned—the greater the self-sacrificing generosity, the more noble and esteemed the host. You now, thanks to your medical condition, have an opportunity to host your own potlatch, turning what is necessary (the disposal of your estate) into another expression of your creative capacity for making meaning and connecting with loved ones in your final days.

Something to consider early on is making a list of where everything you own is. This may sound silly, but a surprising number of people die without letting other people know about old savings accounts, safety deposit boxes, jewelry hidden in some drawer or box, etc. It's amazing how often people hide things of real worth that are only found by chance after their death. Who knows how many valuable objects are inadvertently thrown away? Along with this list, make sure your will has been written just the way you want it, and let your family know it's taken care of so they don't have to worry about it. A will can be as simple as hand-written instructions (called a "holographic will") or as complex as a formal legal document hundreds of pages long. If you have questions about making a will, do not hesitate to ask for help.

As anyone who has ever watched a television soap opera knows, families can dissolve into bitter fighting over wills that are unclear or incomplete. A real gift you can provide to your family is a direct and decisive expression of your wishes for the distribution of your possessions. They may argue anyway, but you will have done your best.

Most family members will enjoy having some special object from your household to remember you by. It can be something large, like a painting or piece of furniture, or small, like a book, watch, or vase. When you decide to whom you're going to give what, write it down and give the list to your caregiver or put the list with your will. It will make the object more special if you also tell the story of how you acquired it and what has made it so meaningful for you. Maybe it was a wedding present, or something from a special trip, or a memento from a particular time of your life. Maybe it's something you created with your own hands—a woodcarving, a painting, a crocheted pillowcase. Whatever it is and wherever it came from, such gifts create a strong emotional bond that will last long after your physical death.

Were *you* given any special objects by elder relatives many years ago as tokens of their lives? Maybe a portrait of a distant relative, or a wedding dress, or a family Bible? If so, you can now choose new people to whom you can pass on these family treasures, to care for during the next generation.

Finally, if you have any pets, let people know how you would like them cared for after you're gone. Although we do not like thinking of our fellow creatures as "things," they are a part of all that which you will leave behind, and in making your estate plans you should include some thought about what you would most like for their continuing welfare. Knowing that they will be lovingly cared for will only make your last days more content.

Reconciliation

All of us at one time or another get into serious disputes with other people. Sometimes the disputes are fairly recent, and other times the quarrels have been going on for generations. Your ability to experience a good death may require you to face these disputes, openly and honestly, and try to reconcile the hurt feelings. You may need to seek forgiveness, and you may need to offer forgiveness. You may need to accept responsibility for painful things you've done to others, and you may need to tell others of painful things they have done to you. The people you have fought with may be right there with you, or they might be far away, or they might have died years ago. Whatever the circumstances, if you make a direct, active effort to resolve the bad feelings, it will tremendously increase your sense of peaceful completion.

A good way to start is to speak with your primary caregiver or someone else you trust very much and tell him or her about the people with whom you've had the worst troubles. Describe as honestly as you can how you got into the fight and what, if anything, you've done to try and resolve it. Then consider what you can do now to effect a greater healing of the situation. This can take the form of a letter, phone call, or personal meeting. Don't expect the other person to automatically respond or reciprocate. If someone refuses your invitation to reconnect, you may have to let the situation go, knowing that you have cleared your side and the rest is out of your hands. More often than not, however, the other person will respond positively to your initiative and will actually appreciate the opportunity to restore the relationship between you. Some situations may require restitution of some kind, by you and/or by the other person. Try to accept your responsibility for what happened, and do your best to make up what was lost.

Sometimes it's not another person with whom you need to reconcile yourself, it's the divine itself. Tish once worked with a woman named Edna who had a calm, mature understanding of her dying situation, and yet spiritually she was struggling terribly with memories of her old childhood religious beliefs about how God punishes sinners. She fell to pieces emotionally every time God was mentioned around her, but she could not say why. She felt confused and scared. Tish asked Edna to think of the Gospels and pick a story about Jesus that she felt related to her. The story Edna chose was from Matthew 26, in which an unnamed lady anoints Jesus with a very expensive oil from an alabaster jar; several other people chastise her for wasting the precious oil, but Jesus forgives her and says she has done "a beautiful thing" and will always be remembered. When Tish asked Edna to describe what she felt was so meaningful in this story, she said it was the element of God's forgiveness—something that Edna had never felt in the whole long span of her life.

She went on to confess to Tish that in childhood she hated her father, a vicious drunk who abused both her and her sister. From the very beginning of her Sunday school days, Edna could not reconcile her father's cruelty with Christianity's teachings about honoring and obeying your parents. When Edna was eight, her father died, and she and her sister moved in with a distant relative and never went to church again. Now, all these years later, Edna was plagued by childhood memories of God's certain wrath for her disrespect for her father. She had been taught as a young girl that death was the time when God would judge those who had been faithful and those who had not. Now she was about to die, and she couldn't help worrying about the punishment awaiting a sinner like herself.

Over the course of several visits Tish and Edna spoke of her religious beliefs and how they had essentially stopped maturing at age eight, while other aspects of her mind and personality continued to grow and mature. The two of them discussed the many different images of God presented in the Bible, including images of God as protector, compassionate companion, and merciful redeemer. They focused in particular on the love Jesus showed for children and his teachings that they be nurtured in faith and love, and never abused. Edna eventually became able to feel compassion for herself as a little girl, replacing her guilt and shame, and she found her religious outlook broadening to embrace God's mercy and grace. She reached the point of being able to express, openly and honestly, her long-simmering anger and resentment toward God. Having done that, she could then allow the deep wound to heal in the light of an expanded faith in God's compassion.

Edna and Tish enacted the story of the lady with the alabaster jar as a means of making tangible these newly emergent feelings of reconciliation and healing. After pouring the precious oil, Edna lit a small votive candle to symbolize her new peace in God's light. She kept the candle alight until she died, ten days later. Her husband had participated in the quiet ritual of reconciliation, and he carefully relit the candle for all to see at Edna's memorial service.

Tending the Soul

As the time of death approaches, people of all beliefs and backgrounds become more interested in asking the big questions of life. Has there been a purpose to my life? Has there been any meaning or value in what I've accomplished? Is there life after death? What will it be like? Is there a Higher Power? Will my character and actions in this life have any impact on what happens after I die?

For people who are members of a faith tradition and have been throughout their lives, it will probably be easy to find a rabbi, minister, or other spiritual guide for consolation and prayer. Most religious organizations have specially trained people who are committed to caring for the dying and their families. If you are part of an organized faith community, you should consider notifying these people so they can become an active part of your care team.

Having said that, a word of caution is in order here. It is well to remember once again that *you* are in charge of who accompanies you in your final days. An individual's spiritual integrity needs to be respected, and if you do not want to have visitors who are coming on behalf of a particular religion, your caregivers and family members should respect those wishes. Particularly if you are confined to a bed or room, you should not be made an unwilling captive to preaching, prose-lytizing, or other unwelcome religious conversations.

On the other hand, if you *are* interested in talking with someone about your spiritual questions and concerns, you ought to be allowed to do so. Even if you have never shown any special interest in such issues before, and even if your family doesn't agree with the direction your desires are leading, you should still have the opportunity to meet with a person who has special training in spiritual counseling. Virtually every hospital and hospice organization in the country has a staff member or consultant who can be quickly brought in to address your needs.

This was exactly the job that Tish held in her hospice group, responding to those patients who wanted to talk with someone about spirituality but who didn't know any specific religious professionals who could help them. Tish's profes-sional title was originally "chaplain," but she quickly had it changed to "spiritual services provider" to reflect more accu-rately the reality of her very diverse work with many different kinds of people, some from traditional religious backgrounds, others brought up in secular families, and a large number of people whose relationships with religion fell somewhere in between. Whenever Tish met someone, she would try to elicit the person's own account of his or her spiritual history, asking questions about family beliefs, early rituals and teachings, and first ideas about the divine. She would ask if the person had ever prayed or meditated, and what that had been like. Allow-ing the dying person's words to guide the process, she would encourage the person to reflect on times when some kind of divine presence was felt, and when that presence was felt to be *lacking*. All of this discussion would gradually lead to a more vivid awareness of the spiritual dimensions of the person's life, allowing for new insights into the possibility of future growth and discovery. There's no predicting where this process will lead, but as Tish found, there is a variety of ways to facilitate and encourage its unfolding. The idea is to focus on the dying person's spiritual comfort, not the caregiver's personal opinion of what that should be.

Taking One's Own Life

Perhaps the greatest spiritual crisis that can face a dying person is the question of whether or not to commit suicide. It's actually quite common for people who have received a terminal diagnosis to consider killing themselves. This anxious pondering can express itself in ideas like: "I'm no use to anyone now," or "What's the point of all this pain and suffering? My life is over anyway," or "It's my life, I can die when I choose." Your family and friends will probably try to dissuade you with well-intentioned reassurances, and if they're worried enough, they may actually try to restrain you to prevent you from ending your own life. Needless to say, this is just about the worst possible pre-death situation that could happen for you and everyone involved.

There are a variety of different beliefs when it comes to suicide near your time of death. Our experience has been that the days and weeks before death can be a time of great learning, "putting it all together," and saying goodbye in powerful ways that speak to the future. These possibilities are always there, *even in circumstances of loneliness, pain, and despair.*

Tish was once called into a household where the wife of the dying person was panic-stricken by her husband's repeated threats to commit suicide. When Tish arrived the wife, a lifelong Catholic named Sharon, burst into tears and said that her husband Paul was going to go to hell and she was going to lose him for all eternity. Paul was not a Catholic, nor had he ever shown any interest in religion, and he kept saying he had a perfect right to take his own life, and no one could stop him.

Sharon begged Tish to tell him he was going to hell if he killed himself.

"He can't commit suicide," she sobbed. "It's forbidden by God!"

Tish asked to talk with Paul for a while, and Sharon showed her to his room. Paul was thin and gaunt and clearly could no longer take care of himself. He was strong enough, however, to sit up comfortably in his wheelchair, and he greeted Tish with a smile and clear, bright eyes. Tish told him that Sharon had invited her to come and talk with him about his threats of suicide. The smile on Paul's face quickly changed to a skeptical frown.

"What do *you* believe about suicide?" he demanded.

Uh oh, Tish thought to herself, *I'm in a tight spot here!* To Paul she said, "We could spend our time together talking about my beliefs, but I'd rather hear about what's been going on for you. How are you feeling?"

Paul replied that physically he was near the end, and he could feel himself getting weaker every day. As for his pain control, he had no major complaints except that it was hard to keep track of so many medications.

Tish asked him what he thought was the worst part of his situation, and he immediately shot back an answer: "I'm bored to tears!"

Paul poured out his frustration about just sitting in his room day after day with nothing to do. He couldn't read anymore, he hated television, and he was tired of relatives fussing around him. He was sick of everything—"I've had it," he concluded defiantly. The implied conclusion was unmistakable. Suicide was a perfectly reasonable response to the situation in which he found himself.

Tish asked him if there was anything special he would like to do, now that his life was coming to an end.

"What do you mean?" he demanded.

"Well, in the time you have left, there are all sorts of possibilities. Is there anyone in particular you'd like to talk to? Or some question you've always wanted to understand better? Or something else?"

Paul was quiet for a moment, thinking. "Okay," he finally said, "if you're a spiritual advisor-type, you must know about the Bible. I am not a religious person and I've never read the Bible." He stared hard at Tish, as if challenging her. "Will you come for an hour every day to tell me the story of the Bible?"

Tish responded in the spirit of a challenge well met. "You're on!"

Over the next two weeks she visited Paul and told him, as best she could, the primary stories of the Bible. He was always very attentive, asking questions every now and then, but for the most part just listening. Tish had the sense that what was going on for Paul wasn't a formal conversion so much as an experience of new learning and broader understanding. He did not suddenly become a Christian (and Sharon continued to fear for the fate of his soul), but Tish believed that what was most important was the fact that in his final days, *Paul kept growing in spirit.* He took the opportunity of dying to confront, openly and honestly, a long-standing conflict in his life. He decided to listen to the stories that were sacred to his wife and to a large percentage of the people in his family, and perhaps for the first time in his life he expressed a latent yearning of his soul. He died a week after Tish's last visit, and Sharon was thankful that he died naturally. She asked Tish to preside at his funeral, which she felt honored to do.

Hummingbirds

This is what makes dying such a mysterious phenomenon— just as your life is ending, surprising bursts of *new* life come into being. Out of the apparent nothingness of your final days, startling transformations occur that open you to broader perspectives and deeper understanding. A "good death" is nothing if not a willing receptivity to experience such transformations, no matter how strange or bizarre they may appear to others. Nothing can give the end of life more meaning than following the lead of your spontaneous creative dreams, visions, and impulses.

One last story. Tish was called to visit an elderly woman named Betty. Her daughter said Betty wasn't religious at all, but she had been "seeing things," and perhaps Tish could help figure out what was going on. When Tish arrived at Betty's apartment, she found a note on the door that said "just walk in." She entered and found a small, dark room that smelled of old food and sickness. As her eyes adjusted to the dusky light, she saw a lady sitting on an old recliner chair, motioning to Tish to come closer. Betty suffered from cancer of the eye, and the right side of her face was badly disfigured. Tish sat down with her, and they began to talk. Betty made no apologies for the "hard life" she had lived, and Tish was amazed at the colorful profanity that filled her description. A regular at all the local bars, Betty had "seen it all," and she didn't care if other people disapproved of how she spoke, or what she drank, or who she slept with. She knew her family considered her a "hopeless drunk" who had failed to live up to the moral code of their religion.

Rather than commenting one way or the other on the moral evaluation of Betty's behavior, Tish asked her what she had been "seeing" that was so strange. Betty's one good eye brightened.

"I've begun to see birds in my sleep," she said. "And I found some of the same kind in a magazine. So I asked Sherry [her daughter] to get me some colored pencils and paper, and I drew pictures of them."

Betty leaned over to a nearby table, picked up a little stack of drawings, and handed them to Tish. They portrayed beautiful, brightly colored hummingbirds, several different varieties flitting among the flowers of a garden. Amazed by the contrast between the brilliant hues of the hummingbirds and the dark drabness of the apartment, Tish asked Betty where she thought the birds were coming from. Betty replied with a question of her own.

"Do you think the spirit has been hidden inside me all along?"

They spoke for a long time about the birds and all that they might metaphorically represent for her. Betty talked about lightness and air, about freedom, and about how she hated her body and its increasingly grotesque condition. She was literally getting lighter and lighter as the days went on. She had all but stopped eating, and her body was physically wasting away. But she kept seeing the birds and drawing pictures of them, and with Tish's encouragement Betty invited her family to look at the pictures, too. Sherry and the other family members were just as astonished and delighted as Tish had been, and the drawings became the surprisingly enjoyable and meaningful focus of everyone's last visit with Betty.

Just before she died, Betty asked to be baptized. Her family was delighted and quickly organized a beautiful outdoor service to comply with her wish. Betty was brought out of her apartment onto the lawn, where holy water was poured over her cancer-ravaged face while her family and friends watched and prayed. It was a very powerful experience for everyone involved, though for Betty her sleeping and waking visions gave it a whole new dimension of significance and value. Whatever its function as a traditional religious ceremony, the baptism took on a surprisingly profound meaning for Betty— as a beautiful bird taking one last bath in the open air and sunshine.

CONCLUSION

Nothing we have recommended in this book requires any special expense, training, expertise, or technology. The caregiving approach we are advocating is as simple as reflecting on your dreams and sharing them with others. Although it can be helpful to have the assistance of a professional therapist, counselor, or dream group, you do not need them to understand your dreams. We really want to emphasize this: *You can understand your own dreams.* All humans are natural dreamers, and all of us have the inherent capacity to make sense of our dreams and learn valuable lessons from them. Each of us is our own best expert when it comes to discerning their meanings.

Challenges Ahead

Far too few terminally ill people in America receive adequate end-of-life care, especially with regard to emotional support. A recent study published in the *Journal of the American Medical Association* found that hospitals and nursing homes, where almost 70 percent of Americans pass their final days, do not provide enough respect, sympathy, and interpersonal warmth for dying patients. People who die at home, either with or without hospice care, fare somewhat better, but even in these cases there were widespread failures of adequate care-giving. The situation is more alarming because, as everyone knows, the large demographic group known as the "baby boomers" is reaching old age, putting even greater strain on a system that is falling significantly short of its goals. Even with all the marvels of modern medical technology, a surprisingly large number of people are not provided with the basic conditions for a good, dignified death.

There are no easy solutions to this crisis. Major improvements will have to be made at many levels of the healthcare system, and much more effort will have to be expended to provide pain relief treatment and other types of comfort to all the people who need it. Beyond that, the *quality* of the way dying people are treated by those whose job it is to care for them must be improved. Dr. Diane Meier, director of the Center to Advance Palliative care, said in a comment on the *JAMA* article mentioned above that "What's very striking is what they say makes for high-quality care. They're talking about being seen as a human being, being heard, being listened to."[45]

Reflecting on dreams in the ways we have described in this book can lead to satisfying precisely those needs identified by Dr. Meier. Dreamsharing is remarkably effective in creating a mutual atmosphere of honesty, respect, and empathy. If our society's goal is to provide better support for the emotional needs of dying patients, a very easy way of making progress toward that goal is to encourage the dying and their caregivers to pay more attention to dreaming. As we've said, no technical training is required to do this, no special expense, no background in this or that school of psychology. All that's needed is an open mind, honest curiosity, and the willingness to discover something new about oneself.

A Summary of Methods

Let's go back over the dream exploration process we have been describing. To begin with, we suggest you reflect on your life as a dreamer. Take the opportunity to go back in your mind to your most memorable dreams, the dreams that, for one reason or another, have stayed in your memory all your life. Maybe you can only remember one or two—that's fine, what's important is opening your awareness to the dreaming aspect of your life. You have always been dreaming, every night of your life. Now you have a chance to think about the dreams you remember as valuable commentaries on your life's strongest feelings, wishes, fears, and hopes.

Next, you can try listening for new dreams. Just by reading this book you will probably experience an increase in the number of dreams you remember. It seems our dreaming imaginations are eager to get our attention, so when we actively welcome dreams into awareness, the response is often quite strong. Keeping a dream journal or diary can be a big help, as the practice of writing out your dreams preserves their memory and allows you to watch the unfolding over a series of dreams of recurrent themes, images, and emotions.

We encourage you to consider sharing your dreams with people you trust (we also encourage caregivers to invite this and, if appropriate, to share their own dreams with the dying person). Talking about dreams is a powerful way of communicating important but hard-to-express feelings. Whether or not your discussion with the other person leads you to find "the meaning" of the dream, you will surely benefit from the open exchange of honest emotion and personal intimacy. Most likely, you will get much more from dreamsharing than that. Sharing your dreams can give you new perspectives you couldn't quite reach all by yourself. Other people's reactions and responses can provide you with alternative possibilities of meaning, enriching your overall understanding of the dream.

As long as the other people always respect the fact that it's *your* dream, their comments can be extraordinarily insightful. Again, we are all dreamers, and we are all capable of serving as trustworthy companions for other people in their personal dream explorations.

Dreamsharing is most powerful and effective when it occurs in an atmosphere of safety and trust, and when it is guided by a spirit of curiosity and open-ended playfulness. Although we do not offer a particular script to follow (spontaneity is of the essence), we do believe that certain questions can be especially helpful in stimulating new insights. These questions include the following:

- Specification: Why, out of the infinite possibilities available, has my dreaming imagination presented me with these particular characters, settings, and activities? What makes these characters, settings, and activities special or distinct in my life?
- What is the most vivid element in my dream, the point of greatest energy, intensity, and vitality?
- Are there any abrupt shifts or changes in the setting, the characters, or the narrative of my dream? Does anything happen suddenly or unexpectedly?
- What is the weirdest, most bizarre, most "counterfactual" element in the dream? Does anything happen that couldn't possibly happen in waking life?
- Are there any notable patterns of symmetry and contrast in the dream? For example, distinctions between male and female, child and adult, kin and non-kin, profane and sacred, good and evil, hot and cold, dry and wet, day and night, up and down, back and front, left and right, white and black, dead and alive, light and dark?

Asking these kinds of questions and seeing where they lead can open up new dimensions of meaning in your dream. Most dreams bring together elements from your past, your present, and your future, so it's worth reflecting on your dream's relevance to each of these periods of time.

Hopefully by now you have recognized the vital need for personal judgment in working with dreams. There is no substitute for your own sense of what is true and what is not, what is more meaningful and what is less meaningful, what is relevant to your situation and what is irrelevant. This can be a difficult point to remember for people who are dying of a disabling disease and have lost the ability to take care of themselves in basic ways. *Even in such conditions,* you are still the best judge of where your dreams are leading you. You may have loved ones who can share your dreams and accompany you part of the way, but ultimately you are the one who must discern in which direction your journey lies.

The Democracy of Dreaming

The potential to experience a powerful pre-death dream is built into human nature. Reports of such dreams have come from a limitless variety of people—women and men, the young and the old, the powerful and the weak, the religious and the secular. Abundant evidence from history and anthropology teaches us that dreams offer a universally accessible means of becoming closer to the sacred. Spiritual dream experiences are not restricted to people with special qualities, training, or social status. It seems that every person has at least the potential to experience a vivid, existentially meaningful dream. Dreaming can therefore be considered a natural wellspring of religious experience, natural in the sense of being an inherent capacity of each and every human being.

When a person experiences a pre-death dream, the benefits often extend beyond just the dreamer. As we've seen several times, such dreams become part of family lore, shared and discussed and treasured for years. Pre-death dreams also act as inspirations for other dying patients who, after hearing a report of someone else's spiritual transformation, become more open to their own dreams and visions.

The overarching claim we are making in this book is that pre-death dreams and visions are regular, healthy occurrences, frequently with very positive emotional consequences for the people who experience them. We consider dreams and visions to be essentially the same in this regard, and we have spoken primarily of dreams because dreaming has a natural foundation in the normal functioning of the brain-mind system every night when we go to sleep—this makes dreaming a more familiar experience than visions, which occur in a waking state and which happen much less frequently than dreams. Still, both dreams and visions share in the expression of deep creative powers that lie within all people, and we are calling for greater awareness of this potential. We are not the first to do so; everything we have said has deep roots in Western civilization, and indeed in the history of many cultural traditions. This is truly ancient wisdom.

More than fifteen hundred years ago, Synesius of Cyrene, a philosopher and religious leader from North Africa who combined the wisdom of Plato with the new teachings of Christianity, wrote a beautiful treatise on the subject of spiritual dreams. In this work he gives an eloquent statement of the democratic power of dreaming, and we would like to close our book with his resonant words:

> The dream is visible to the man who is worth five hundred *medimni,* and equally to the possessor of three hundred, to the teamster no less than to the peasant who tills the boundary land for a livelihood, and to the galley slave and the common laborer alike, to the exempted and the payer of taxes. It makes no difference to the god whether a man is a citizen or a newly bought slave. And this accessibility to all makes divination [through dreams] very humane; for its simple and artless character is worthy of a philosopher, and

its freedom from violence gives it sanctity. . . . Of divination by dreams, each one of us is perforce his own instrument, so much so that it is not possible to desert our oracle there even if we so desired. Nay, even if we remain at home, she dwells with us; if we go abroad she accompanies us; she is with us on the field of battle, she is at our side in the life of the city; she labors with us in the fields and barters with us in the market place. The laws of a malicious government do not forbid her, nor would they have the power to do so, even if they wished it, for they have no proof against those who invoke her. . . . A tyrant could never enjoin us not to gaze into dreams, at least not unless he actually banished sleep from his kingdom. . . . To her then we must go, woman and man of us, young and old, poor and rich alike, the private citizen and the ruler, the town dweller and the rustic, the artisan and the orator. She repudiates neither race, nor age, nor condition, nor calling. She is present to every one of us, everywhere, this zealous prophetess, this wise counselor, who holdeth her peace.[46]

APPENDIX

Resources for Caregiving for the Terminally Ill

No one should die without being given every chance possible for a good death. Fortunately, services for caregiving for the terminally ill are widely available, and in fact are expanding both nationally (in the United States) and internationally. Every local community has its own network of service providers, and we suggest you look to the following sources for information to discover what's offered in your area:

YOUR LOCAL HOSPITAL
The medical staff at virtually every hospital in America now has training in end-of-life care, and they can provide you an immediate source of professional guidance.

CLINICAL SOCIAL WORKERS
Many hospitals have clinical social workers on staff, and these people have special training in developing comprehensive care teams for terminal patients and their families and friends.

COUNCILS ON AGING
Most counties have a council on aging that aims to provide clear, trustworthy public information about issues that confront people when they are preparing for death.

NATIONAL HOSPICE ORGANIZATION
This group can put you in touch with the nearest hospice provider to where you live. Hospice workers are trained to help dying people with nursing, home healthcare, counseling, medications, Medicare and insurance documents, legal referrals, and chaplaincy services.

VETERANS ADMINISTRATION
The VA offers a wide array of end-of-life services for people who qualify as veterans or military dependents.

RELIGIOUS GROUPS
For those people who are seeking religious guidance, or are at least comfortable with some degree of spiritual content in their care, local religious groups are another helpful resource for counseling and comfort.

DREAM GROUPS
If you are especially curious to learn more about your dreams, you can contact the International Association for the Study of Dreams (IASD) to find individuals and/or groups in your area who are experienced in dreamwork and willing to talk with people like yourself.

ACKNOWLEDGMENTS

Our greatest thanks go to the generous people who shared their dreams with us. Though we have modified details of their stories to preserve their privacy, we have tried to honor the truths of their experiences. We are grateful for everything we have learned from several educational institutions, especially San Francisco Theological Seminary, Princeton Theological Seminary, the University of Chicago Divinity School, and the Graduate Theological Union. Several colleagues have provided invaluable guidance in the development of our work, and we want to single out for special appreciation Lewis Rambo, Roy Fairchild, Ruth Ann Clark, and Sandra Brown from San Francisco Theological Seminary, Mary Ann Scofield from Spiritual Directors International, Mary Taverna from Hospice of Marin, the late James Loder from Princeton Theological Seminary, and Jeremy Taylor from Starr King School for the Ministry. The wonderful people at Beacon Press, including Amy Caldwell, Gayatri Patnaik, Tom Hallock, Kathy Daneman, Pam MacColl, Lisa Sacks, and Jennifer Yoon, have taken as much care of our project as any authors could hope. Our families have been right with us throughout the writing of this book, supporting our efforts and encouraging our dreams—thank you Hilary, Ned, Michelle, Alex, Kevin, Dylan, Maya, Jake, Alec, Conor, and Amanda.

ACKNOWLEDGMENTS

A word about the spellings of our last name. They are variants of the same family name, that of the Rev. Peter Bulkeley, a Puritan who left England in 1635 and founded a new church community in what became Concord, Massachusetts. Tish and her husband, Ned, are part of a family branch that dropped out the first "e." Kelly, their eldest son, now spells his last name with the additional "e."

NOTES

1. Although there is no consensus on the exact definitions of "religion" and "spirituality," in this book we use both terms to refer to the recognition of powers that transcend human control or understanding and yet have a formative influence on, and discernible presence within, human life. "Religion" refers to a relatively more formalized appreciation for those powers, and "spirituality" to a relatively less structured engagement with them.
2. 2 Cor. 4:16–18 (Revised Standard Version).
3. Van de Castle 1994; Miller 1994; Lincoln 1935; Kelsey 1991; Jedrej and Shaw 1992; Young 1999; Ong 1985.
4. Hobson, Pace-Schott, and Stickgold 2000.
5. For more on Freud and Jung, see Bulkeley 1997.
6. Doniger 1998, p. 59. Italics in the original.
7. Jung 1968, 1974, 1974; Revonsuo 2000.
8. Lakoff 2001.
9. Foulkes 1999; Hobson, Pace-Schott, and Stickgold 2000.
10. Domhoff 1996, 2003.
11. Domhoff 1993.
12. Van de Castle 1994.
13. Dement and Vaughn 1999.
14. This estimate is based on the admittedly limited findings of Hall and Van de Castle.
15. Reported in an interview to Kelly.
16. Hesiod 1973, vv. 211–212.
17. Ong 1985, pp. 93–94.

18. Augustine 1870, pp. 272–276.
19. Eccl. 5:3, Ps. 73:19–20, Is. 29:7–8, Deut. 13, Jer. 29:8–9, Zech. 10:2, Gen. 28, 32, 38–42, Joel 2:28.
20. Kelsey 1991; Sanford 1982; Savary, Berne, and Williams 1984; Taylor 1983, 1992; Hall 1993; Clift and Clift 1988.
21. Lakoff and Johnson 1980, p. 5.
22. Lakoff 2001, p. 274.
23. Thomson 1994.
24. Thomson 1994.
25. Pace-Schott et al. 2003; Moffitt, Kramer, and Hoffman 1993.
26. Jung 1974, p. 41.
27. French and Fromm 1964, p. 24.
28. Cartwright and Lamberg 1992, p. 269.
29. Hobson 1999, p. 117.
30. Hobson 1999, p. 152.
31. Revonsuo 2000.
32. Plato 1961, *Crito* 43d–44b.
33. Hollan 2003, p. 70–71.
34. Fourtier 1972, p. 1.
35. Sanford 1982, p. 59–60. We have made slight modifications to Sanford's text to include additional relevant details.
36. Sanford 1982, p. 60.
37. Wulff 1997, pp. 147–150.
38. James 1958, p. 384.
39. Smith 1965, pp. 59–62.
40. Hartmann 1995, 1998.
41. Bosnak 1989.
42. Bosnak makes no comment on the different spellings of "shute" and "shoot," and we wonder if there might be different meanings or feelings attached to the variant spellings.
43. All translations are from Salisbury 1997.
44. The change in Dinocrates' bowl echoes the boulders of Ruth's dreams, which change over the course of several dreams from immovable impediments to enticing invitations. For a recent discussion of the maternal qualities of Perpetua's dreams, see Davis (in press).
45. Teno et al. 2004.
46. Synesius 1930.

REFERENCES

Augustine. 1870. *The Works of Aurelius Augustine, Volume XIII: The Letters of Saint Augustine*. Translated by J. G. Cunningham. Edinburgh: T&T Clark.

Bosnak, Robert. 1989. *Dreaming with an AIDS Patient*. Boston: Shambhala.

Bulkeley, Kelly. 1997. *An Introduction to the Psychology of Dreaming*. Westport: Praeger.

Cartwright, Rosalind, and Lynne Lamberg. 1992. *Crisis Dreaming*. New York: Harper Collins.

Clift, Jean Dalby, and Wallace B. Clift. 1988. *The Hero Journey in Dreams*. New York: Crossroad.

Dement, William C., and Christopher Vaughn. 1999. *The Promise of Sleep*. New York: Dell.

Domhoff, G. William. 1993. The Repetition of Dreams and Dream Elements: A Possible Clue to a Function of Dreams. In *The Functions of Dreaming*, edited by A. Moffitt, M. Kramer and R. Hoffmann. Albany: State University of New York Press.

———. 1996. *Finding Meaning in Dreams: A Quantitative Approach*. New York: Plenum.

———. 2003. *The Scientific Study of Dreams: Neural Networks, Cognitive Development, and Content Analysis*. Washington, D.C.: American Psychological Association.

Doniger, Wendy. 1998. *The Implied Spider: Politics and Theology in Myth*. New York: Columbia University Press.

Foulkes, David. 1999. *Children's Dreaming and the Development of Consciousness*. Cambridge: Harvard University Press.

Fourtier, Millie Kelly. 1972. *Dreams and Preparation for Death*. Ann Arbor: University Microfilms.

French, Thomas, and Erika Fromm. 1964. *Dream Interpretation: A New Approach*. New York: Basic Books.

Hall, James A. 1993. *The Unconscious Christian: Images of God in Dreams*. Mahwah: Paulist Press.

Hartmann, Ernest. 1995. Making Connections in a Safe Place: Is Dreaming Psychotherapy? *Dreaming* 5 (4):213–228.

———. 1998. *Dreams and Nightmares: The New Theory on the Origin and Meaning of Dreams*. New York: Plenum.

Hesiod. 1973. *Theogony*. Translated by D. Wender. New York: Penguin Books.

Hobson, J. Allan. 1999. *Dreaming as Delirium: How the Brain Goes out of Its Mind*. Cambridge: MIT Press.

Hobson, J. Allan, Ed Pace-Schott, and Robert Stickgold. 2000. Dreaming and the Brain: Towards a Cognitive Neuroscience of Conscious States. *Behavioral and Brain Sciences* 23 (6):793–842.

Hollan, Douglas. 2003. Selfscape Dreams. In *Dreaming and the Self: New Perspectives on Subjectivity, Identity, and Emotion*, edited by J. M. Mageo. Albany: State University of New York Press.

James, William. 1958. *The Varieties of Religious Experience*. New York: Mentor.

Jedrej, M. C., and Rosalind Shaw, eds. 1992. *Dreaming, Religion, and Society in Africa*. Leiden: E. J. Brill.

Jung, C. G. 1968. *Man and His Symbols*. New York: Dell.

———. 1974. General Aspects of Dream Psychology. In *Dreams*. Princeton: Princeton University Press.

———. 1974. On the Nature of Dreams. In *Dreams*. Princeton: Princeton University Press. Original edition, 1948.

Kelsey, Morton. 1991. *God, Dreams, and Revelation: A Christian Interpretation of Dreams*. Minneapolis: Augsburg Publishing.

Lakoff, George. 2001. How Metaphor Structures Dreams: The Theory of Conceptual Metaphor Applied to Dream Analysis. In

Dreams: A Reader on the Religious, Cultural, and Psychological Dimensions of Dreaming, edited by K. Bulkeley. New York: Palgrave.

Lakoff, George, and Mark Johnson. 1980. *Metaphors We Live By.* Chicago: University of Chicago Press.

Lincoln, Jackson Stewart. 1935. *The Dream in Primitive Cultures.* London: University of London Press.

Miller, Patricia Cox. 1994. *Dreams in Late Antiquity: Studies in the Imagination of a Culture.* Princeton: Princeton University Press.

Moffitt, Alan, Milton Kramer, and Robert Hoffman, eds. 1993. *The Functions of Dreaming.* Albany: State University of New York Press.

Ong, Roberto K. 1985. *The Interpretation of Dreams in Ancient China.* Bochum: Studienverlag Brockmeyer.

Pace-Schott, Ed, Mark Solms, Mark Blagrove, and Stevan Harnad, eds. 2003. *Sleep and Dreaming: Scientific Advances and Reconsiderations.* Cambridge: Cambridge University Press.

Plato. 1961. Crito. In *Plato: Collected Dialogues.* Edited by E. Hamilton and H. Cairns. Princeton: Princeton University Press.

Revonsuo, Antti. 2000. The Reinterpretation of Dreams: An Evolutionary Hypothesis of the Function of Dreaming. *Behavioral and Brain Sciences* 23 (6).

Salisbury, Joyce E. 1997. *Perpetua's Passion: The Death and Memory of a Young Roman Woman.* New York: Routledge.

Sanford, John. 1982. *Dreams: God's Forgotten Language.* New York: Crossroad.

Savary, L. M., P. H. Berne, and Strephon Kaplan Williams. 1984. *Dreams and Spiritual Growth: A Christian Approach to Dreamwork.* Mahwah: Paulist Press.

Smith, Huston. 1965. *Condemned to Meaning.* New York: Harper & Row.

Synesius. 1930. *The Essays and Hymns of Synesius of Cyrene.* Translated by A. Fitzgerald. London: Oxford University Press.

Taylor, Jeremy. 1983. *Dream Work.* Mahwah: Paulist Press.

———. 1992. *Where People Fly and Water Runs Uphill.* New York: Warner Books.

Teno, J. M., et al. 2004. Family Perspectives on End-of-Life Care at the Last Place of Care. *Journal of the American Medical Association* 291:88–93.

Thomson, Sandra A. 1994. *Cloud Nine: A Dreamer's Dictionary.* New York: Avon Books.

Van de Castle, Robert. 1994. *Our Dreaming Mind.* New York: Ballantine Books.

Wulff, David. 1997. *Psychology of Religion: Classic and Contemporary.* New York: John Wiley & Sons.

Young, Serinity. 1999. *Dreaming in the Lotus: Buddhist Dream Narrative, Imagery, and Practice.* Boston: Wisdom Publications.

Printed in the United States
By Bookmasters